Books by J. Frank Dobie

Out of
the Old Rock

Out of
the Old Rock

J. FRANK DOBIE

LITTLE, BROWN AND COMPANY · BOSTON · TORONTO

LIBRARY OF CONGRESS CATALOG CARD NO. 71–186971

FIRST EDITION
T04/72

We are grateful for permission to include the following previously copyrighted essays in this collection:

"Out of the Original Rock" from the 1962 Denver Brand Book. Copyright © 1962 by the Denver Posse of the Westerners. Reprinted by permission of the Executive Committee of the Denver Westerners.

"Ed Bateman, Wildcatter" from the December 1948 issue of *Holiday* magazine. Copyright 1948 by the Curtis Publishing Co. Reprinted with permission from *Holiday*.

"A Cowboy Preacher and His Book" from the October 1942 issue of *The Cattleman*. Copyright 1942 by *The Cattleman*. Reprinted by permission of *The Cattleman*.

"Don Quixote of the Six-Shooter" from the May 1942 issue of *New Mexico Magazine*. Copyright 1942 by *New Mexico Magazine*. Reprinted by permission of *New Mexico Magazine*.

"Roy Bedichek" and "Walter Prescott Webb" from *Three Men in Texas* edited by Ronnie Dugger, published by the University of Texas Press. Copyright © 1967 by the *Texas Observer*. Reprinted by permission of the University of Texas Press.

"Tom Lea" from *Tom Lea, a Portfolio of Six Paintings* by Tom Lea, published by the University of Texas Press. Copyright 1953 by the University of Texas Press. Reprinted by permission of the University of Texas Press.

*Published simultaneously in Canada
by Little, Brown & Company (Canada) Limited*

PRINTED IN THE UNITED STATES OF AMERICA

Preface

THIS book is a bequest. In his will Frank Dobie, mentioning books he had planned to make and then hoped one of his two literary executors or someone designated by them would make after he was gone, listed among other "makings" a "book of character sketches." He had considered the subject for a long time. In his copy of *This Is New Mexico* he wrote: "I don't know whether my sketch of Clay Allison in this book will ever get into another book or not. I think of a collection of characters of the Southwest and West, in which Allison might be one." The signed note is dated June 8, 1948.

The books Frank sent to press are filled with characters, as I increasingly realized when sketch after sketch that would have fitted into *Out of the Old Rock* had to be discarded because it had appeared in another of his books. He seldom told a story orally or in print without limning a person. This was one means of "fleshing out" a narrative. "The best of talk among men," he wrote, "is meaty with anecdotes of character, specimens of human behavior." His own talk and his writing were much of a piece.

Frank valued his ability to bring life to a name, but considered it inferior to his mother's. Of her gift, which was exercised only in talk, he wrote: "It was her way of hitting off characters that I can't equal — just an incident or a saying or a glimpse that lighted up the whole figure."

My primary task in bringing people together between book covers was to establish principles of inclusion. Here our editor, Larned G. Bradford, was a great help. There would be no Robert Frost, no Carl Sandburg, no Charles M. Russell, but only people of the Southwest. Time as well as geography entered in. With small exception, the people in this book were known to Frank. He is the mirror that reflects them. Within these lines, I have presented as great a variety of men as possible.

Among my early decisions was to call the book *Out of the Old Rock* and to put the sketch Frank titled "Out of the Original Rock" first. Why *original* I do not know. Only this once do I recall his having used the word instead of *old,* with *rock.* For the title I preferred *old* because not infrequently Frank both spoke and wrote about persons "out of the old rock." That I wanted to make the book at all was due in part to my desire to give what permanence a book may afford to the sketch placed last, "E. Douglas Branch, Singularísimo"; and E. Douglas Branch was not "out of the old rock."

All the character sketches have appeared elsewhere, some in two or three places: in Texas newspapers as a Sunday column that ran for twenty-five years without a break; in *Southwest Review;* in journals of the Southwest and West; in introductions; and in other people's books. I am particularly grateful for permission to include in *Out of the Old Rock* essays previously published by University of Texas Press, Encino Press, University of Nebraska Press, *Southwest Review* and the Texas Folklore Society.

The sketches were written over many years. Present time has become past, but tenses have been left as they were. Dating the sketches seemed a clumsy interference; changing the tenses, an impertinence.

Always my thanks to Willie Belle Coker, custodian of the Dobie Collection in the University of Texas Library. This time I am more than ever indebted to her, since she supplied some writings that I had forgotten.

BERTHA McKEE DOBIE

On Waller Creek
Austin, Texas

Contents

Out of
the Old Rock

Out of the Original Rock

I NEVER knew him, but from what Bob Montgomery tells me, his Uncle George McGehee (uncle by marriage) must have been one of the most individualistic individuals belonging to old-time Texas. Bob (Dr. R. H.) Montgomery teaches economics in the University of Texas and used to make a comedy out of legislators investigating him for having modern ideas. I wish I could present him in conceptions of life side by side, simultaneously with George McGehee, as a picture reveals grass on one side of a fence and bare ground on the other side. George McGehee was born before the Alamo fell and died opposing change to the last; Bob Montgomery, his great admirer, has spent the best years of his life trying to understand change and think out the wisest ways to meet it.

In Scotland the family name was spelled Mac (or Mack) Gehee. McGehee is pronounced McGee. In 1833 two brothers, John Gilmer McGehee and Thomas Gilmer McGehee, representing a numerous clan in Alabama and Georgia, landed at the mouth of the Brazos River in Texas. They had come by way of Pensacola, Florida, where they loaded a schooner with lumber. They sold the lumber to Stephen F. Austin's colonists and then prospected up the Texas Colorado River for land, choosing the area around Bastrop. They went back home and the next year returned overland in wagons with a company of settlers. It was January of 1835 before they began settling in what is now Bastrop County.

Thomas Gilmer McGehee had a young wife and an infant daughter. Texas was already rising against Mexico. That fall John McGehee was so severely wounded in the battle of Concepción, which resulted in occupation of the Alamo by a part of the Texas army, that he was still at home recovering when the Alamo fell. Mexican agents were doing their best to stir up Indians against the settlers, and Thomas McGehee was throughout most of the war scouting the country west of the Colorado River on the lookout for raiding parties. On February 5, 1836, his first son, named George Thomas, was born at Bastrop — just thirty days before the Alamo fell on March 6. When news of the fall of the Alamo reached the Bastrop settlement, most of the able-bodied men had left to fight the Mexicans, Thomas McGehee among them. His brother John, still crippled from his wound, did what he could to help kinspeople and others set out east on what is called the Runaway Scrape — running from Santa Anna's army.

Thomas McGehee's wife, Minerva, had a pair of small, three-year-old oxen named Dick and Ben. Her husband had ridden away on Bill, the only horse owned by the family. Minerva got Dick and Ben hitched to a rickety two-wheeled Mexican cart, loaded on corn, quilts and other necessities, put little George and his sister where they could not fall out, and, walking beside the oxen to drive them, struck east through the mud. Eighteen hundred and thirty-six was a notably rainy year. Minerva had to leave behind the nice bedclothes, books, paintings and other luxuries brought from Alabama. She owned a small slave girl, and the girl walked with her. She had no money and, besides, there was no place to buy anything. Daily her provisions grew scantier. Some days the oxcart moved only a few miles. It was still inching east when word of the victory at San Jacinto came. The little oxen pulled Minerva's cart back to the Bastrop settlement.

Thomas McGehee had located his headright league of land (4,428 acres) on the San Marcos River, where the Blanco runs into it. It was not until 1846 that he moved his family to this land, thirty-five miles from Bastrop. He built the first substantial house and farmed the first field of consequence in what became Hays County.

George, a big boy now, was sent on horseback back to Bastrop for some papers. Before he left, his father said, "You are riding a good horse. If you see any Indians, you can outrun them." On the way back, George saw what he took to be Indians under a tree away off to one side of the road. They did not move. Keeping hid in the tall grass and in timber, he approached nearer and discovered that the Indians were twelve buffalo hams that some white hunters had hung from tree limbs. Buffaloes on the prairies were numerous; they were to play an important part in George's life.

He had some schooling at Rutersville, where a Methodist academy was established. His people were strong, "spiritually minded" Methodists and their home was always a home for preachers. The good books he was reared on at home, along with the good people who reared him, gave him an outlook and a sense of values that accompanied him through life and solaced him when he was an old man sitting by the fire and lighting his pipe with spills of rolled-up paper that he kept handy beside his chair.

By the time he was sixteen years old, he was a man in ability and independence. It must have been before this that he went with his father on a scout for strayed horses clear up into the Llano country. He remembered the date as 1844. There were no settlers at all in that region then. As he told the story repeatedly many years later, one morning, just as the sun was coming up, they rode up on a granite hill for a look over the country and saw Mexicans and Indians panning for gold in a stream. They were not seen by the miners, and the McGehees .did not investigate. They rode all day southwest, crossing the Pedernales River, and that night camped at The Narrows on the Blanco River, reaching home the next day.

Along in the 1880's George McGehee, well fixed now, became interested in stories circulating about the Lost San Saba Mine, called also the Lost Bowie Mine, and in renewed hunts for it. He decided that the men he and his father had seen panning for gold were at the original Lost Spanish Mine, in the Llano, rather than the San Saba, drainage. He tried to retrace the horseback ride he had made more than forty years before. He was confident that if he could ever see the creek, especially from the granite hill where he and his father had watched the gold panners, he would recognize it. Now the country was all fenced and settled and growing up in brush. He made trip after trip looking for the granite hill and the creek. He was sure at first that the creek ran north into the Llano; later he decided that it must run south.

Finding the creek and "mine" became a passion with

him. He hired geologists and he leased mineral rights of ranches; he kept men familiar with the terrain of a vast country riding. Late in life he told Bob Montgomery that he believed he had spent a quarter of a million dollars on a search that extended over many years. Perhaps he was counting in what he might have made had he not been spending so much time on the chase.

George T. McGehee claimed that when he started riding out and noticing, back in the days of the Texas Republic, there were no mesquites in central Texas and mesquite grass was up to a man's stirrups. About 1852, when he was sixteen years old, he became a kind of scout attached to the United States Army. Jefferson Davis, Secretary of War, was having a route surveyed to the Pacific Ocean that was later followed in great part by the Southern Pacific Railroad. George McGehee's business was to provide buffalo meat for the surveying crews and the soldiers guarding them.

While in this business he met a man from New York who was buying buffalo robes, and he contracted to furnish him one thousand at $10 apiece. He hired seven Mexicans to skin, dry and scrape the hides, and in one season killed 988 buffaloes in Hays County, mostly on the prairies between San Marcos and Wimberley. He freighted the cured hides to Harrisburg (or maybe even Galveston) and then went with them by ship to New York, where he collected cash for them.

He took the money to Moline, Illinois, and bought new wagons with it. The wagons were rafted down the Mississippi to New Orleans and there loaded on a boat for Galveston. Here George McGehee bought oxen, hired drivers and set out across Texas with his train of new wagons. Money was mighty scarce in Texas then, but the demand for new wagons was strong, and before George McGehee got to his home on the San Marcos he had sold out and had $20,000 in cash. He was a rich man according to standards of the day, and for the rest of his life was considered rich.

He went through the Civil War as a private. In later years, when nearly every ex-Confederate was called Colonel or Major, he claimed that he was the only private in the Confederate army, making him "the army."

When he was thirty-six years old he married Sarah Woods. They never had any children but adopted a daughter and helped various children out of big families of kinsfolk through school. One of these was Bob Montgomery, whose mother was a sister to Sarah Woods McGehee. Bob lived with the couple for nearly ten years in San Marcos, going to school and teaching. According to Bob, Uncle George hardly weighed more than 120 pounds, all wire, fire and vitality, while Aunt Sarah got up to around 200 pounds, a monument to placidity.

After Bob Montgomery got a Ph.D degree and was drawing a university salary, he went to Uncle George one day and told him he wanted to pay back what he had been out for his keep. "No," Uncle George said, "you pass it on to another boy." As fully a dozen graduates of the University of Texas know, Bob Montgomery followed George McGehee's behest.

Until almost the last, Bob says, "Uncle George was the best hunter I have ever seen" — and Bob has hunted with the best. "He had an old .38-caliber, octagon-barreled rifle. He knew what he could do and not do with it and never missed a buck running or standing. He scorned city hunters who wounded deer and let them get away."

He and Aunt Sarah had a big house in the middle of a block in San Marcos. He had no use for city water and irrigated a fine orchard and garden from his own well. He drove a horse to a surrey long after automobiles became rather common, but finally got one. He had a great barn right there in town and kept two cows that Bob Montgomery milked. He took delight in giving away extra milk and butter, would not have thought of selling any town produce. If somebody to whom he had presented fruit or vegetables thanked him, he would say, "If you wasn't welcome, I wouldn't give it to you." The city tried to get him to connect with the sewer line, but a private septic tank satisfied him. For a long time after a toilet was installed in his house he continued to use the barn privy. When he had a telephone installed he did not want such a concession to corporations regarded as a precedent.

He served in the state legislature and led in legislation to have state prisoners work and learn trades by which they could make a living after being discharged from the penitentiary. He read books and had a considerable collection on criminology, along with sets of Dickens, Mark Twain, and Alexandre Dumas and histories of the French Revolution. He and Major George W. Littlefield led in getting a bronze monument honoring Terry's Texas Rangers erected on the capitol grounds in Austin.

Despite public-spiritedness, he did not in his heart believe in the ever increasing organization of society or in courts. "Any man," he said, "who can't defend his own property, his own honor and his own ideas with his own rifle does not deserve to have property, honor or rights."

About 1910 he bought 2,000 acres of level black land in the San Patricio country west of Sinton, in south Texas, and began the expensive operation of getting it cleared and farmed. While he was spending a great deal of time and money on Sodville, as he named this acreage, he invested $25,000 in an oil company organized by a banker who claimed to have valuable leases in Mexico. One time when George McGehee came back to San Marcos from Sodville he learned that the oil company was a fake and that his wife, who had invested some of her money in it, and other investors were preparing to sue.

He belonged to the church and went to church, but he used strong language when he felt like it, which was frequently. Now he said to Aunt Sarah, "You damned socialists will sue and you won't get a thing. Watch me." She watched, but did not see him when he left home one day with that old octagon-barreled rifle. When the banker saw him, the banker was looking into the rifle barrel. The banker had trust in lawyers and court procedure but he knew that George McGehee would make his own word good. He wrote out the check for $25,000 as suggested by George McGehee. Uncle George had the cash from the check in a little black satchel when he came home.

"There my money is," he said. "I guess you damned socialists will sue."

He did not like the way the "damned socialists" were extending public education. He invented and patented a combination root-plow and tree-puller to clear out the mesquites at Sodville, where he had many Mexicans hired. One time he came back to San Marcos storming. "It's bad enough," he said, "that they tax me to educate Mexican children. Now the school is getting a bus to take them to Sinton. They'll get a little education and be as worthless as whites" — meaning they would not come back and work for him at 50 cents a day.

Before daylight every morning he would build a fire in the cookstove and put on a pot of coffee. Then while he was waiting for the coffee to boil he would drink a toddy. At ninety he said, "If I had not drunk a toddy every day since I was three years old, I'd be a hundred and fifty now."

Many people thought him rich and rough. He was neither. He could be courtly. He liked to walk with a cane. He had a collection of canes, among them a gold-headed one that had been given him by Sam Houston. It was for state occasions, when he dressed for the part.

On September 13, 1926, he ran a stalk-cutter all day on a Sodville field, came in, put the stalk-cutter under a shed, cleaned up, got in his car and headed for San Marcos. At San Antonio he telephoned ahead that he was coming. This was unusual. He arrived about midnight. He said, "This world is no fit place for a white man to live in." Then he walked over to his cot, for he would not sleep on a bed, lay down and died. He lacked about five months of being ninety-one years old.

Nobody knew what he had done with the $25,000 in cash collected from the banker–oil promoter; probably he had spent it on Sodville. After he died, the San Marcos house was almost destroyed by hunters for hidden money. His estate turned out to be very modest.

He belonged to the simple, honest times of two old-timers in one of Bob Montgomery's stories. One went to the other to borrow a thousand dollars. The second man said he could have it. Then the question came up as to who should keep the note. "You keep it," the lender said. "I know you owe me, and having the note will remind you when it is due." That was settled.

On the day stipulated, the borrower brought the thousand dollars and paid it. Now the question came up again as to what should be done with the note. "I've paid it," said the borrower, "and don't have no more use for it. You keep it." The lender took it. He didn't have any use for it either, but somebody had to keep the note.

At the end of his true and beautiful book on Kelly Blue, a primitive artist of Texas, William Weber Johnson quotes from a letter written by Kelly Blue on the death of an old horseman. The climax of the letter is out of Job:

"At destruction and famine thou shalt laugh: Neither shalt thou be afraid of the beasts of the earth. For thou shalt be in league with the stones of the field and the beasts of the field shall be at peace with thee."

The quotation fits George McGehee. He was out of the old rock.

Beeville Talk

WHEN I was young I began associating all I could with old men to learn from them, to garner their experiences, their knowledge, their narratives and sometimes wisdom. I enjoyed their fellowship, sucked up life from it. For the same reasons I find myself now seeking younger men. Nearly all the old-timers I started out with are gone, but one who ranks high among them still regales and fills me whenever I see him.

That is Jim Ballard of Beeville, Texas — my old stamping ground and my mother's home for over thirty-five years. I have never known a man with a better memory for things worth remembering, an apter way of expressing himself, or more logic in relevance. He likes old times and stories that have something of the mystery of life; also, with his one eye he can see farther through the befuddlers of the new times than a lot of two-eyed editorial writers and public speakers can. He admires close observers. While he talks, he whittles a tiny ranchman's boot out of soft wood, and when his visitor rises to go, gives him the boot.

He was born at Hallettsville, Lavaca County, in 1872. He is little and eager. For decades he was a druggist. For a while he was postmaster, a Republican appointee. A great-grandfather was professor of Greek and Latin in William and Mary College in Virginia. His Grandmother Hallett was as positive a character as has stood among the women of Texas. "Biscuits," she told him, "were called Billy Seldom when I was young, whereas unvarying cornbread was called Johnny Constant." I could listen to him talk all day about his Uncle James Ballard of Hallettsville.

This uncle could read fourteen languages, and he considered most of the inhabitants of the region too ignorant to waste his time on. He would get up at three o'clock in the morning, light a lamp, and, holding it in his right hand and a book in his left, pace the floor, studying and reading. He surveyed lands, very accurately, and one year while he was on a surveying expedition, citizens, without consulting him, elected him county judge. Shortly after the election, he overheard a man say that nobody without enough knowledge of law to hold a license to practice should be county judge. He straightway read enough law to pass the bar examination, but after one term in office would not stand for reelection.

He could add three columns of figures at a time and was often called upon to make out tax reports for officials who could hardly trust themselves to add one column correctly. His customary reward was a new hat. He habitually wore an old one with holes in it through which his hair stuck out. In time he accumulated a whole shelf of new hats that he never put on. He did not like to wear new clothes, either, and his old ones were as ragged as his hat. He owned farmlands that he rented out on shares, for a third of the corn crop and a fourth of the cotton. One year after a renter had filled James Ballard's corncrib and stacked up a pile of corn outside and covered it with a tarpaulin, he drove up with another big load and announced that he had several other wagonloads to bring.

"Take it back. I don't want any more corn," James Ballard said. "Do what you want to do with it." A daughter was incensed that he would not have it hauled to town and sold at the market price.

He was more than six feet tall and habitually stepped over the courthouse yard fence instead of walking through the gate. It was in his nature not to conform — and if I were adding to the beatitudes, I would say, "Blessed are the nonconformists."

While Jim Ballard was still a small boy, an orphan, his Uncle James said to him, "Your ignorance is a reflection upon me. I suggest that you join my school." He was teaching an assortment of children in the Odd Fellows' Hall. They were not in grades. Some were learning their ABC's on slates. One or more had advanced to the stage of computing the thickness of the wall of a soap bubble at the point of bursting. Jim agreed to join these learneds provided he might quit when he wanted to. One night he heard Uncle James tell his wife that if all the pupils stayed through the term and he collected tuition due on them, he would make $150 that year. Jim Ballard considered that "not enough reward for knowing fourteen languages and being able to figure out the thickness of a soap bubble," and he quit.

He himself is a character without being an eccentric. He relishes the blunt speech of an old-time rancher at whose home he used to stay while deer hunting. One afternoon while they were sitting in the kitchen drinking coffee, the rancher looked up and said, "Well, we'll get the news now. Sarah Braxton is coming in."

"There's no need to rile her," the rancher's wife said.

"I just said we'll get the news now," the rancher repeated.

Within a minute after Mrs. Braxton entered she began relaying scandal on a neighbor.

"Nobody has to believe everything he hears," the rancher interjected.

At that, Sarah Braxton drew into her shell. After she had been silent a few minutes, the rancher said, "What's the matter? Why don't you talk?"

"I was talking and you called me a liar."

"No, all I said was you needn't believe everything you hear. But I generally mean what I say and am mean enough to say it."

Another old-timer who had come through tough times among tough men was asked by Jim Ballard how he managed to escape trouble himself.

The old-timer replied, "I never had any trouble with anybody, I never got into anybody else's troubles, and I rode a fast horse."

"You knew Wash Barker?" Mr. Jim asked me.

"No, only by reputation. He claimed to have seen the Rock Pens, where Spaniards hid thirty-one mule loads of silver."

"He killed several men and kept free," Mr. Jim said, "but finally killed one man in a way that would have hanged him sure or sent him to the penitentiary for life. He skipped the country, got out west, had a picture made showing him dead, and had the picture sent back home. For twenty-five or thirty years his problem was to keep himself dead. He finally came home on assurance that court action would not be taken. He told me about some of his experiences while on the dodge.

"I asked him if in all that time he had not seen anybody from south Texas who recognized him or whom he recognized. 'I saw Dave Walton's saddle on a horse in front of a saloon in Lordsburg, New Mexico,' he said. 'I kept on riding.'

"He hadn't seen Dave Walton for five or six years. He recognized the saddle. Perhaps he got close enough to see that it was made by Tom Sonley or Paul Bauer, the Beeville saddlemakers. He wouldn't have had to see any name, though, if he had ever looked at the saddle with his keen eyes. He told me about coming up to a saloon at night at a time when he knew that officers were on his trail. He had an idea that maybe one or more of them had passed him and got ahead of him. He dismounted and felt the horses at the tie-rack to see if they were sweaty. He felt the saddle blankets under the saddles. Caked sweat meant as much to him as warm sweat."

One time Jim Ballard went to hear an intelligent man make a speech on an issue about which there was strong feeling — which does not necessarily mean strong thinking. A heckler interrupted, "I can't hear what you are saying."

The speaker replied, "I can make you hear, but I can't give you understanding."

It's hard to indicate in print the kindness and good nature pervading even the sharpest criticism of life in one of Jim Ballard's anecdotes. He tells about some know-it-all skeptic who boasted, "There are some things in the Bible I just can't understand. They bother an inquiring mind."

"The part of the Bible bothering you," Jim Ballard replied, "is what you do understand."

This recollection brought up W. J. Stayton; "Bull" Stayton, he was commonly called. He was an extensive trader in horses and bulls. One day while I was still a small boy, my father took me with him in a buggy to Mr. Stayton's ranch, east of the Nueces River from our ranch, to buy some bulls. On the road he told me that Mr. Stayton was an infidel. According to Jim Ballard, a preacher went to Mr. Stayton to buy a team of buggy horses. He liked the horses and liked the price but told Stayton, "I'm just afraid to buy your horses."

"Why?"

"You don't believe in God."

"That's true, not in the kind of God you talk about."

"Well," the preacher went on, "if you don't believe in God, then I can't believe anything you say about these horses."

"Oh, yes, you can," Stayton came back at him. "You can take my word better than you can take the word of those men in the Amen corner. They can lie and then turn around and get forgiveness for lying. I have nobody to turn to. I have to tell the truth."

We got to talking about a character unnecessary to name. "Some people," Jim Ballard pinned him down, "won't go to a funeral unless they can be the corpse."

Maybe this isn't original. Coming in at the right place, it is just as good as if it were. It makes me think of my brother Elrich's style. Elrich is the wit of the whole Dobie tribe. I wish I could write as well as he sometimes talks. One difference between us is that while he does not dislike neckties any more than I do, he almost never wears one. He spoke the other day about a fellow wearing a collar so stiff and high he had to strain to spit over it.

Jim Ballard used to have a barber friend in Beeville who was a philosopher. The barber liked to preach a sermon on a text he had originated: "You can't take anything with you from the grave that you don't leave here."

I told Mr. Jim that this has more implications than what another homemade philosopher said in reply to the question as to how much a certain rich man had left: "Everything."

"Now," Mr. Jim said, "you take old Captain A. C. Jones. Of course, I don't know where he went when he left this world, but he left some good here, and I guess he took some good with him. Beeville has had good men since, but no *papacito* like Captain Jones. He didn't have to get out of his buggy to see anybody when he came to town. All he had to do was stop in the shade and in a little while his buggy would be surrounded by men. He did more than anybody else to bring the railroad. That was in 1885, I believe. Before the state supplied textbooks to schoolchildren, they were sold here in Beeville by my drugstore. Every fall Captain Jones would come to me and say, 'Jim, if there is any child who does not have money to pay for school books, if the parents don't have the money, you deliver the books anyway and charge to my account.'"

"You mean just any child?" Jim Ballard would ask.

"I mean any child in the county — white, Mexican, Negro."

Textbooks that Captain Jones gave away, Mr. Jim says, might amount to $150 a year or more.

For a long time Mr. Jim has been an officer in a bank.

When the building was renovated several years ago, the old-time portraits of Captain A. C. Jones and other pillars of the bank were taken from the walls and stored in the attic. That wasn't Mr. Jim's idea. The features of a good man say something sometimes. The heirs of a certain dead father fell to quarreling over their portions and took their case to a lawyer who was a family friend. He told them all to come to his office at a certain hour on a certain day. Meantime he had a photograph of the father enlarged and hung in the office in a conspicuous place. After the heirs arrived, he left them alone — facing the portrait. Before long the chief troublemaker among them came out and told the lawyer that the picture had put them to thinking about their father and they had settled their differences.

Some of the men Jim Ballard likes to talk about are humble folk. One time, when he and I were agreeing that a genuine Mexican is much to be preferred to a "Latin-American," he recalled that in the old days of credit business a Mexican tenant farmer, coming in during the cotton season to pay his bill, would seldom ask, "How much do I owe you?" He would not say, "I want to pay my account." He would say, "I want my name." He had given his name, his honor; his name was in the hands of another man. He wanted it back. One time a Mexican who owed about $35 moved east several counties. Seven years went by, and the account had long been charged off as a loss. Then one morning a young Mexican, the son, came into the store.

"My papá he is daid," the young man said. "He tell me you have his name. He say for me to geet back his name. I come now for eet. Please to let me have eet."

"I had a hard time finding the old account," Jim Ballard said. "After it was paid, I told that young Mexican that if he ever got stranded, no matter if he was in New York, to send me a telegram and I'd send him money to come home on.

"I've heard that down in Mexico in the old days after a man had gambled away his last cent, he still had another bet coming. He might be nothing but a peon wearing *guaraches* [sandals]; likely he was. He could go to the proprietor of the gambling place and demand a stake for one more bet. This was called the 'bet of honor.' If he won, he paid his debt immediately. If he did not win, he paid when he could — and got back his name."

Jim Ballard asked me if I was ever on the Charco much.

"No."

"Well, when I went there, a native told me that in order to qualify for citizenship in that section, a man had to find three hogs asleep and then steal the middle one without waking up either of the other two. Oh, yes, the hogs were razorbacks. They sleep light, mighty light."

There are three kinds of narratives in which Jim Ballard excels — the kind involving the longbow, accounts of old-time shortwits, and just little happenings that silhouette characters and phrases. Often he gets into the realism of humanity — narratives that cannot be printed on account of living descendants. For instance, there was a certain pioneer who left his wife with six or seven children; after she had managed to rear them well, he came back broke and wanting a home. She would not see him. But there is no marrow, blood, heart, humanity in summary. Jim Ballard never summarizes; he always deals in specifics.

One time when he entered his philosophy-friend's barbershop he noticed two or three loungers, besides the three barbers, all idle. A stranger walked in. He hung his hat and coat on the rack and as he placed himself in the middle barber's chair said, "Well, it's the biggest fish I or anybody ever caught out of the Nueces."

"How much did he weigh?" the attending barber asked.

"One hundred and twenty pounds, and I caught him on a twenty-pound line."

About this time a rancher came in and prepared to sit down in the first chair.

At sight of an addition to his audience, the stranger repeated, "Yes, that catfish weighed one hundred twenty pounds."

The rancher said nothing but the barber about to wait on him asked, "Where was it you said you caught that fish?"

"Out of the Nueces River."

The rancher said, "I've lived on the Nueces River all my life, and I've never heard of any catfish weighing anything like that."

"Well, you have heard of it now," the stranger said.

"I was fishing in the Nueces just the other day," the rancher said, "and when I went to pull out a heavy line with a big hook on it I felt something that made me think at first I had hold of an alligator. But it wouldn't move and then I decided it was a log. I jerked the line around a little and dreckly the thing gave way from its fastening and wasn't any trouble at all to pull in. It was an old rusted lantern, and the peculiar thing was it was still burning."

"I don't propose to be called a liar," the stranger said with some energy.

"Nobody has called you a liar, so far as I've heard," the rancher said. "I just said I fished a lantern up out of the Nueces and it was still burning. But I'll tell you what I'll do. I'll blow out my lantern if you'll knock sixty pounds off your catfish."

Among entertainers and men ready with the right word whom he has known Jim Ballard ranks Jasper Miller at the top. One time, long ago when wide-open saloons flourished in Beeville, Jasper Miller burst out of a saloon just as Jim Ballard was passing it.

"What's up?" Jim Ballard asked.

"I can't play to that spinner," Jasper Miller replied.

It turned out that Jasper Miller had been sitting at a table in the saloon with two other men playing dominoes. After a few hot words — mighty few but plenty hot — had passed between the two, one grabbed his chair and crashed it down on the table. It wasn't a good "spinner" to play to.

Jasper Miller always maintained that a man can't get anywhere "unless he has Lady Luck around his neck." He said that one night at a ranch house he was in a poker game at which each of four players started with a cupful of shelled corn — white grains worth two bits apiece. Luck was against him from the start. After two hours he saw that his cup was about empty. With a *con permiso* he withdrew and went out through the kitchen.

There he saw a Mexican worker and asked him where the corn was kept. The Mexican said that it had not been gathered yet, that all the corn was still in the field. Jasper Miller knew the lay of the land and didn't need a light to go by. A corn field came right up to the backyard. He stepped into it, felt an ear on a stalk, pulled it, shucked it, and as he walked back into the house shelled off the grains and half-filled his pocket with them. He sat down, got into the game again, manipulated the cup under the table and transferred a generous number of the newly shelled grains into it. Then he looked. The new corn was all red. Later, he said, the Mexican told him that when they gathered the corn not another red ear showed up. "Lady Luck shore didn't have her arms around my neck that night," he said, as Mr. Jim reported.

Our talk drifted to sayings designed to baffle the tongue. A tongue twister I grew up on is: "Three long, slim, slick sycamore saplings." Then there is the one all children delighted in, perhaps still do for all I know: "Peter Piper picked a peck of pickled peppers. Where is the peck of pickled peppers Peter Piper picked?" These are easy compared with one of Jim Ballard's: "Theophilus Thiscus, the great thistle sifter, in sifting thistles thrust three thousand thistles through the thick of his thumb." Mr. Jim also gave me this out of his childhood: "I saw Esau kissing Kate. The fact is, we all three saw, for I saw Esau, he saw me, and she saw I saw Esau."

"I don't know absolutely," Mr. Jim said, "what is the longest sentence in the English language that can be spelled and read backwards and remain the same as when read forward, but I have always heard it is this one: 'Able was I ere I saw Elba.'"

Edgar Kincaid, the ornithologist who probably knows more about Texas birds than any other man, was with me once calling on Jim Ballard. He asked when the white-winged doves that make a canopy of sound over

Beeville first came there. Mr. Jim wasn't sure, but he said, "I've been living in this house sixty years, and the same redbird made a nest in a tree right off the gallery here for twenty-five years."

Edgar Kincaid asked him how he knew it was the same redbird.

"Why," Mr. Jim said, "he got to know me and every morning he'd call out to me, 'Jim, Jim, Jim.'"

You have to hear a voice imitating the redbird's to get that.

"Mr. Jim," I said, "I've been doing what the kindergartners call 'research' on stingy cowmen. Now I ask you for a word on the stingiest cowman you've ever known in this cow country."

"I'd rather not name him," Mr. Jim said, laughing the bright, quiet laugh that's a part of his nature. "I knew one cowman who wore a bigger hat than anybody else to indicate how broadminded he was. He was a noted accumulator. All he wanted, he said, was what land he had a title to and what joined him."

Well, according to my values, no factory maker or sermon maker is equal as a benediction to society to a vivid, witty talker just sitting in a chair and talking.

A quarter of a century and more back the Beeville *Picayune* ran a column under a figure resembling Jim Ballard's with the right hand upraised over the title "Years Ago: The Truth, the Whole Truth and Nothing But." The weekly newspaper of Hallettsville is now rerunning these columns. Here is a sample, an ancient folk tale made fresh by retelling.

Two men got to discussing the effect of marriage on a man. One declared he had never known a married man who was boss in his own house. Once in a great while, he said, you would find one talking loud around the house when company came, but after the company left he would pipe down mighty low.

The two men decided to make a test. Early the next morning they loaded a wagon with chickens, hitched up two good horses to the wagon and started out to locate a boss. They were to give away a chicken if the woman was boss. If a man was found to be boss, they would give him a horse.

After they had nearly run out of chickens they drove up to a house where the husband sat in a rocking chair on the front gallery reading the sporting news while his wife was hanging out a hard day's washing. They stopped and told the man the purpose of their visit.

"Fine," the man said. "Where is my horse?"

"Step out to the wagon and choose which one of the team you want," they told him.

The big boss walked right out, looked the pair of horses over and said he'd take the little sorrel. Just then his wife appeared and told him she thought he'd made a bad choice.

"I know what horse I want," said the husband. "You go on back and tend to your own business."

"Yes, honey," replied the wife, "but we really need the larger horse, that black one."

He wouldn't yield. She called him to one side and spoke a few words for his ear only. Then Mr. Married Man walked back and said that after thinking the matter over he'd decided to take the big black horse after all.

"Now," said the owners, "all you get is chicken."

Another man I always went to see in Beeville, whenever I visited my mother, was Judge James R. Dougherty. For a third of a century he was Mister Jim to me as to many others. Usually we talked in his office, occasionally in his home. His mellowness, his richly stored mind, his wide and deeply assimilated experience with men and affairs, the mixture in him of imagination and intelligence, all combined to make his talk some of the best that has blessed my life. There were limitations to Mr. Jim's sympathies, but his intellect transcended the lines drawn by sects, provinces, and political parties.

For many years he had not practiced law, but the tradition of his speeches to juries is still green. When he began practicing, the main business for country lawyers was criminal cases. Killings were much commoner then than now, and any man between San Antonio and Brownsville who got into a "difficulty" wanted Dougherty and Dougherty to represent him.

Chrys Dougherty died years ago, but the firm name was never changed. Mr. Chrys was a Presbyterian in religion and Mr. Jim was a Catholic; few brothers were ever more devoted to each other. After Mr. Jim became wealthy from oil speculation, he could be counted on to help Protestant institutions in his hometown as well as his own church.

He told me about one civil case that gave him a deal of satisfaction. According to Texas law, a navigable stream is state property; any stream not navigable belongs to owners of the land through which it flows. A quarter of a century or so ago, oil was struck in minor quantities near the Frio River on a ranch in McMullen County.

According to my recollection, a well was drilled almost in the bed of the Frio. When the State of Texas set up a claim to the mineral rights of the Frio River, the oil company developing the field and the rancher engaged Mr. Jim to represent them. The question of ownership turned on whether the Frio River was ever navigable. Old-timers were called into court to testify. Mr.

Jim wanted evidence antedating any living memory. He came to the library of the University of Texas to search the Spanish archives, for he read as well as spoke Spanish, and consulted Dr. Eugene C. Barker of the history department. Dr. Barker advised him to consult Teran's diary (of the early nineteenth century). He consulted it and found an entry reading something like this: "On such and such a date we camped on the Rio Frio. It is *mal nombrado* [poorly named]. There is little water; it is not *frio* [cold]; what water there is *es casi potable* [is hardly drinkable]." That quotation from Terán's diary decided the case in favor of Mr. Jim's client.

Mr. Jim made me see as nobody else ever made me see my mother as she was before I was born. He said that one spring just before my Uncle Frank Byler and my step-grandfather, Friendly Dubose, started to Kansas with a herd of range horses, there was a neighborhood picnic to which he and Chrys went. They were just boys. My mother's people were ranching on the Nueces River in Nueces County; the Doughertys lived at San Patricio, which was not far away on the same river. Mr. Jim said that he saw my mother and my Aunt Fannie riding spirited horses. They were fair and auburn-haired and seemed to him then the most beautiful young ladies he had ever looked upon. Then and all his life he called my mother, who was a little older, "Miss Ella."

Newly born colts could not be taken on the trail, and Uncle Frank Byler gave him a colt belonging to a mare that would start up the trail next day. He and Chrys managed to get the colt home, raised it and afterward rode it.

Mr. Jim cherished the flowers and wild animals that belonged to the land to which he also belonged. He said that when he was a child his father came in one day early in the spring and told his wife to bring the children to see the most beautiful tree he had ever beheld. Then he drove the family in a buggy to a crossing on the Nueces River a short distance above San Patricio, where a lone huisache tree was covered with golden flowers — the first to be observed in that part of Texas. It had come up from Mexico. There are millions of huisaches in Texas now.

In those times when the huisache tree (*Acacia farnesiana*) was a novelty, the land was replete with deer and wild turkeys. Mr. Jim used to tell of going to a camp just abandoned by hunters and seeing numbers of fine bucks and turkeys left to rot and feed the buzzards. I don't know if he ever hunted or not. For years he was active in preserving wildlife, not just game, on his ranches.

We were talking in front of the fireplace in his home when he said, "I got a copy of the *Oxford Book of English Verse* not long ago. I have been slightly familiar with Mr. Wordsworth a long time, but I had never read the 'Ode on Intimations of Immortality' before. You know its theme — how man loses the freshness of things that quicken youth all over. It's true that experiences are not so fresh as they used to be, but reading this great poem, the freshness of boyhood on the Nueces came back to me.

"I experienced again the first green of the elms, the hackberries and other growth along the Nueces bottom. The mesquites put out a little later. There is no green like this first green. Viscount Grey of Fallodon used to invite his best friend — Salisbury, it seems to me the friend was — out to his manor in England to see the first green. It won't last longer than a week. The English green is beautiful, I know, but it can't be more beautiful than the green along the Nueces, up and down the river from old San Patricio, that I knew as a boy. The way the little longhorn calves, as ring-streaked as the lambs whose mothers had gazed at the striped poles Jacob set up at the waterings, jumped around in the green is a part of the memory."

Right after I talked with Mr. Jim on the first day of October, 1938, I wrote down one of his stories. It has come into my mind hundreds of times since while I have listened to whippoorwills or poor-wills in the night.

"About 1903," Mr. Jim said, "before the St. Louis and Brownsville railroad built into the Rio Grande Valley, Lon Hill told me I ought to buy some land down there. He said much of it was for sale cheap and would be worth good money someday. You knew Lon Hill, didn't you, with his long hair and Indian eyes? He was a character.

"Well, after court recessed at Brownsville, I went to San Benito, got a buggy and a Mexican *mozo* [servant] and struck out to look at a tract of two thousand acres away out in the brush somewhere. We drove all afternoon and about sundown came to a hacienda owned by an old Mexican ranchero. All around his house were other houses, just *jacales* [cabins] made of adobe and poles with thatched roofs. They were pretty good little houses. The patriarch said they were all occupied by his children and grandchildren and maybe great-grandchildren. He asked me to stay all night, saying there was a jacal at my disposal. I thanked him but told him that I had come prepared to camp.

"My mozo made a fire and cooked a little bacon and

coffee, and after we had eaten we sat by the fire a while, for the weather was cold. I enjoyed smelling the mesquite smoke coming out of the jacales. Have you ever noticed how far away you can locate a Mexican jacal by the smell of mesquite smoke after dark? While we were sitting there, a whippoorwill began calling down in the *resaca* [a bayou-like creek].

"*El per-di-do,*" the mozo said. [*Perdido* means lost.] Then he told me the story of the bird. There in the night by the campfire, the cries of the bird and the story both sounded beautiful to me. I can't remember what happened to the bird in the story, but the bird did something that made him an outcast among the other birds, and ever since being cast out he has been proclaiming *per-di-do, per-di-do, per-di-do* [I am lost, I am lost, I am lost].

"Yes, I bought the land, two thousand acres at three dollars an acre. Lon Hill sold it for me not long after at five dollars an acre. It went up to hundreds of dollars an acre later — but that's not the story of el perdido.

"Some Mexicans say that the bird is called per-di-do because that is what he says, and he does say 'per-di-do' just as plainly as he says 'whippoorwill.' Others say that he is called perdido because he is almost never seen and is always lost in the night when he cries out his cry of the lost."

Lon C. Hill, the man who sold the land to Mr. Jim Dougherty, was a lawyer at Beeville before, with the advent of the first railroad into Brownsville, he became a land promoter in the lower Rio Grande valley. He helped make the valley "magic." He knew the juries, Mexicans and land-hungerers and a lot besides. He was part Choctaw Indian, and wore his hair long enough to hang down over his shoulders; his shaggy eyebrows were harmoniously long.

Well, one day back in prohibition times, Lon C. Hill got on the train at Brownsville to ride east. He carried, according to his habit, an oblong black satchel containing his usual traveling equipment: a clean shirt, a nightshirt, a bottle of whiskey and a six-shooter.

Soon after the train started, he picked up his black satchel and went back into the Pullman smoker. He sat down, putting the satchel at his feet. Two other men were in the smoker. A very brisk young man entered and without taking time to become acquainted addressed himself to Lon C. Hill.

"I am a prohibition enforcement officer," he said. "Here are my credentials." He displayed a medallion worn on the underside of his coat lapel. "A lot of liquor is being crossed from Mexico and carried into the United States," he went on briskly. "I'll just take a look inside that satchel of yours."

"I don't believe I'd like for you to," Lon C. Hill said.

"I ask you to open the satchel," the agent persisted.

"I'm not a-going to do it," Lon C. Hill said.

"Then I'll open it," the young man announced.

"Oh, if you persist," Lon C. Hill said quietly.

He was bending over opening the satchel and reaching into it. In a flash he raised the six-shooter. Pointing it at the young man, he said:

"Young man, this is either the last satchel I'm a-going to tote or the last one you are a-going to open."

The young man backed off.

This anecdote about a one-time Beeville "character" was told to me by Bill Kittrell, of Dallas, one of the best storytellers I have encountered during almost a lifetime of appreciating storytellers. Maybe it didn't happen exactly this way.

Anybody who enjoys his reputation for being odd, saying odd things, being contrary to conformity, comes to be almost under an obligation to say and do the unusual. The late Dr. Lee Edward Parr of Beeville acquired the reputation of being a character, and he did his best to live up to the reputation.* Oddity of character does not flourish in an atmosphere of conformity and orthodoxy. I do not have any strong feeling that the world is going to the devil much faster than it has been accustomed to going during the past thousand or two thousand years, but I do sincerely wish for more eccentrics and heretics.

One cold, wet night back in the horse-and-buggy days, Dr. Parr drove 20 miles west to the Nueces River on an urgent call. After examining the patient, a man, Dr. Parr asked his anxious wife if she had any whiskey. She had — well hidden away, evidently. She brought out a quart — not a cheating fifth — and the doctor ordered, "Now fix him a hot toddy, pretty strong." She boiled water on the wood stove in the kitchen and after a while brought the toddy in a tumbler. "I'd better taste it first," Dr. Parr said. He tasted it and then gulped it all down. "That's a little too sweet," he said. "Fix another." She brought back a second toddy. "Let's see how it tastes," the doctor said, taking it. Again he tasted, again swallowed the whole prescription. "You got it a little too

---

* Dr. Ernest Miller of Beeville and Miss Jean Dugat of the Beeville High School have been collecting anecdotes about him. Those that follow are from their collection.

strong," he said. "Try again." After sipping the third toddy, he said, "That's just right. Let him have it."

But whiskey was by no means a universal sovereign with him. One time during prohibition days a man entered his office with a self-diagnosis. "I'm sick," he said, "and need a prescription for a pint of whiskey." Without even grunting — and he could grunt — Dr. Parr examined the patient thoroughly from tongue to stomach. "Yes," he finally concluded, "you are pretty sick. A bottle of castor oil will fix you up." He handed the startled patient a prescription for the same, and collected the usual fee for an office visit.

One day while sitting at the fountain counter in a drugstore drinking coffee, Dr. Parr was accosted by a man who asked, "What is good for a cold?"

"Time," he retorted. After the man went out, he explained to a friend coffeeing with him, "I'm not giving free advice."

During a cold epidemic, word got out that Dr. Parr was laid up. A friend who was worried about his health in general had started to call at his house when she met him on the street with a heavy scarf about his neck. "Why, Dr. Parr," she exclaimed, "what are you doing out in this weather with that bad cold?"

"Spreading it around to make more business," was the reply.

He was imperturbable. Not long after he had given his daughter a spirited buggy horse he was sitting in a café drinking coffee when a man hurried in to report that the horse was running away with her. He continued drinking his coffee slowly. "Aren't you going to do anything?" the man asked.

"She started the horse," Dr. Parr replied. "She can stop him."

After he acquired an automobile, he became an inveterate tinkerer with it. Somebody very often had to tinker with most early-day automobiles. Every morning on his drive from home to the office, Dr. Parr could be seen stopping in the shade of a big mesquite tree and tinkering, presumably "adjusting the carburetor." On the way home in the late afternoon he usually stopped under the same mesquite for further tinkering.

He ordered a $60 special carburetor, and when it was delivered to him, paid the price in cash and then asked, "How do you adjust it?"

"Why," the agent replied, "it's made so that it does not need adjusting."

"Then I don't want it," Dr. Parr announced. "Just give me back my money and send the carburetor back to the company that made it. Any carburetor that's worth anything needs adjusting."

One of the times when he backed his car into another he got out to investigate the damage. Seeing that the other car had its windshield broken, he commented, "Oh, that's all right. It's summertime."

One day he stopped so abruptly while driving down the main street that a woman driving behind him could not help running into his car. He got out to inspect the damage. "If I had known you were going to stop, I would not have run into you," the woman said.

"Madam," he replied, "if I had known you were going to run into me, I would not have stopped."

On a fishing trip to the coast it was discovered after camp was made that whoever was responsible for chuck had neglected to bring milk and eggs. Dr. Parr, who always wanted cream in his morning coffee, did not fail to comment on the lack. Several hours later when he walked into camp after a tour of fishing, he noticed a bucket of milk. "Where did that come from?" he asked.

"A farm woman gave it to me and refused any payment," a proud rustler replied.

"Then you should have asked for eggs, too," Parr commented.

The kind of hard-boiled averseness to the sentimental often sublimated in the aphorisms of George Bernard Shaw helped along the Parr reputation for originality.

Bob More, Man and Birdman

ROBERT Lee More was born at Decatur, Texas, September 16, 1873. After twenty-seven energetic growing years in this community he entered the employment of D. Waggoner and Son and moved to Vernon, Texas. There, having been with the Waggoners without interruption during the intervening decades and having for years been responsible for the immense operations of the Waggoner Estate, he died on September 6, 1941.

One June day in 1888, Bob More, then in his fifteenth year, came to the house at noon from plowing in his father's field on the edge of Decatur. After dinner, while lingering a few minutes on the front gallery before going back to the plow, he noticed a black vulture fly into a brush pile on the creek. At noon the next day he saw the same vulture fly again into the same brush pile. When on the third day he saw the performance repeated, he went to investigate. He thought the vulture might be after a snake. Instead, he found a nest with two eggs in it, about the size of turkey eggs, semi-ivory in color with reddish-brown splotches on the big ends, one of the two being, characteristically, more heavily marked than the other. He took the eggs. That night he blew their contents out in a crude way. Thus began the dominating passion of his life, the great collection of bird eggs that he was constantly adding to until the day of his death.

This collection contains the eggs of around 750 species of birds and, including duplicates, aggregates between twelve and fifteen thousand eggs. A third of the birds represented have their eggs in the original nests — *in situ*. About 150 birds are mounted. Every egg is scientifically marked, according to the plan of the American Ornithological Union. Record books with corresponding numbers give the date and place of discovery, name of collector, species of bird, and description of the nest with number of eggs in it and their condition.

The specimens range in size from the egg of an ostrich to that of a hummingbird; in rarity and value, from eggs of the extinct passenger pigeon and a precious example of the mighty California condor's, to those of the commonest species. They are arranged to show all sorts of variations in color, shape and number pertaining to a single species, and to reveal the whole panorama of the egg world. The collection is said to be the finest in America west of the Mississippi River. It is certainly one of the outstanding private collections in the world.

Half a century and more ago there were not many country communities in Texas where a boy's interest in natural history would find encouragement — except from nature itself. Young Bob followed his interest alone; indeed, throughout his life, except on red-letter days when some ornithologist visited him, or when on some trip he encountered a "bird man," Bob More pursued that interest by himself. But the Decatur community, in Wise County, included among its pioneer families — mostly from the Old South — an unusually large percentage of individuals who might look with sympathy upon any scientific, literary or historical activity. Clarence R. Wharton, who became one of the foremost lawyers and historians of Texas, was a farm boy in the community. Its most distinguished citizen, perhaps, was Colonel William Hudson Hunt, highly cultivated, richly experienced, with a fine library in his home on Cactus Hill, where his daughter Belle, later married to Samuel A. Shortridge, grew into a poet and prose writer. One of Bob More's boyhood friends was Cliff D. Cates, who in 1907 published his *Pioneer History of Wise County* — one of the best and most civilized county histories of Texas. Other community chroniclers were Dot Babb, who had been an Indian captive and who wrote *In the Bosom of the Comanches,* and Colonel R. M. Collins, historian of the Civil War. About two years ago Bob More wrote me to be sure to trail down the diary of Major W. H. Cundiff, an odd and picturesque character of early-day Decatur.

The civilized friend in this community who introduced the boy to an ornithological magazine and other natural history literature seems to have been J. A. Donald, an eccentric surveyor and draftsman ten years his senior. For knowing the land, depend on a surveyor. The two often scouted together. Donald had a collection of bird eggs, kept in a very orderly manner, that Bob eventually acquired.

With the passion for learning about birds and for collecting new eggs surging in him, Bob often left the house, without notice, before daylight to explore all day alone. His father, Charles More, merchant, farmer, rancher, and flour-mill promoter, had lost most of his

property during the great drouth and depression beginning in 1886. Now, at fourteen, Bob's schooldays were
over. In the yard, back of the family home, was a room
that had been occupied by a servant. Fortunately — perhaps — for the young bird-egg collector, it became vacant just as he was needing a museum room. He utilized
it, carefully arranging his eggs and nests in boxes. Later
he got hold of some old showcases; then he graduated
to sectional bookcases. Finally, after he had lived in
Vernon for some years, an office building which was
erected for the Waggoner Estate headquarters was designed to include a large, windowless room, with proper
cases for preserving and displaying his collection.

Oology may be defined as that branch of ornithology
which treats of the shapes, sizes, coloration, et cetera, of
bird eggs, together with their relation to nests and the
nesting habits of the birds. Besides setting him on
his way to become one of America's foremost oologists,
the collecting of that pair of black vulture's eggs in
1888 seems to have marked a turning point in Bob
More's whole career. He quit school in this year, but at
night he read Blackstone, in time becoming well versed
in law, particularly as applied to land and contracts. He
gave up farming to become a delivery boy for a grocery
store. One day somebody brought into the store a mudhen that had been shot. Bob took it and mounted it.
Well preserved, that mudhen is in his collection today.
He had read his lessons on taxidermy carefully.

Lincoln, it has been said, did not go to the White
House because he lived in a backwoods log cabin, but
because he got out of it. Bob More did not deliver gro-
ceries very long before he went to work in the abstract
business for Will A. Miller. Soon he knew more about

making abstracts than his employer, and began abstract-
ing on his own hook, in partnership with John H. Cates,
who continues the business today.

"We were partners for ten years or more," John Cates
told me, "and during all that time we never had a mis-
understanding or a settlement. Bob was a good draftsman and as neat and orderly as he was energetic and
good-humored. 'Rory O'More' — witty, laughing, rol-
licky, honorable hero of ballad and novel by Samuel
Lover — was the nickname everybody knew Bob by in
those days. When he went fishing, first as boy and then
as young man, he never threw a hook into the water
until he had explored out the territory for birds and bird
eggs. He kept a record on all his eggs. There wasn't a
crooked bone in his hide. About the time I married he
went to work for Tom Waggoner at a good salary. 'I
want to give you my share in the business as a wedding
present,' he said. That's the way we dissolved partnership."

While "Rory O'More" was maturing in Decatur, one
of his sidelines — he always had sidelines — was running
the local "opera house." Often he was so busy during
the day that only at night could he put up posters advertising coming attractions. Late one night Tom Waggoner, who with his father had ranches on two sides of
Decatur, was driving home in a buggy with his boss,
ranch manager Tom Yarbrough, when he saw a man
with a lantern mopping away at a billboard. "What's that
fellow doing at this time of night?" Tom Waggoner
asked.

"He's putting up opera house signs," Tom Yarbrough
replied.

"Who is he?"

"Oh, it's Bob More."

"Keep your eye on him," Tom Waggoner concluded. "We might need him someday."

Dan Waggoner and his son W. T. (Tom) had tens of thousands of cattle grazing in the Indian Territory when, toward the end of the century, the government gave them notice to vacate. Under the leadership of Tom Waggoner — the father died in 1902 — the Waggoners began buying large tracts of land to the south of Red River in Wilbarger and contiguous counties. Tom Waggoner badly needed a land man to perfect his titles. It is related that Tom Yarbrough persuaded Bob More to take the job, and that the first question Waggoner asked him was, "What can you do?"

"Well, I can dig postholes," Bob More replied, "but you'll lose money on the deal."

His work in perfecting titles took him all over the country on the trails of missing heirs. Wherever he went he looked for birds and bird eggs. He could survey as well as abstract, and he became intimately acquainted with every hill, swag, flat, creek, field, break, gate and trail of the more than half a million Waggoner acres. Gradually the business of the ranch was placed in his hands. Oil development on it following World War I increased his responsibilities mightily, especially after 1923, when the holdings of Tom Waggoner's children were combined to form the Waggoner Estate. Under Bob More's managership, Three D gasoline, from the Waggoner refinery at Electra, became as well known as the same brand on Waggoner cattle. He was responsible for the Waggoner Pipe Line Company — and he went on studying birds and collecting bird eggs. He never attended a race at Arlington Downs, the track established halfway between Fort Worth and Dallas at a cost of $2,000,000 — which was Tom Waggoner's pride. The Waggoner acquisition in 1931 of a 160,000-acre ranch in New Mexico gave Bob More another bird land to explore. Here he watched antelope increase as eagerly as he watched Rio Grande wild turkeys multiply on the Texas ranch.

In 1925 he wrote to another collector of bird eggs: "I have been collecting for thirty-seven years and am just as enthusiastic as when I started." It was during the twenties that he was most energetic in filling out his collection. To a man who offered him $750 for his California condor egg, he replied: "It is not for sale at any price." Only seventy-eight eggs of the California condor are known to exist in the world, and very few of the birds, which nest in the most inaccessible crags and cliffs, are extant. In 1929 he wrote: "I am especially interested in filling out the duck family, and I would blame near commit murder to get a set of Little Brown Crane eggs." He got them before long.

"I never sell," he wrote again, "but do quite a lot of exchanging and give away a great many eggs." As a matter of fact, when he got down to boxing eggs to send away, he generally gave more than he had promised. His haste in packing occasionally resulted in broken shells; if so, he replaced them. He gave freely to museums.

An egg was not just an egg to him. Concerning a cassowary egg that he received the year before he died, he wrote the donor: "I have one in my collection that was laid in captivity, but this is very different. A bird in its natural habitat means a whole lot. I certainly appreciate this specimen." The confusion of records passed on by some sellers and exchangers of eggs made him resolve many years ago "to confine myself to exchanges of my own taking for eggs taken by the person I am exchanging with . . . I like to divide my sets up with good reliable collectors."

He would drive a thousand miles to take with his own hands a nest that he might have bought for two or three dollars. Perhaps a hundred species of clutches in his collection were taken from the Waggoner acres in north Texas, which he was constantly traversing. When he got out to the Waggoner ranch in New Mexico, he stayed on the alert for eagle eggs. He could drive very fast and look over the land at the same time. But when with his friend and associate, R. B. Anderson, he would surrender the wheel so that he might look for birds without hindrance. He might see "sign" beside a road nearly anywhere, stop and walk a mile or two off to locate a bird's nest. He found many of his nests in fence posts. If he traveled a certain road every day during the laying season, he would stop daily at each nesting post to examine the eggs. In the vicinity of cliffs, he would get out of the car and walk along bluffs examining the ground for eagle droppings. He had made and carried with him a harness and rope to enable him to scale or climb down steep places to reach the nests.

He blew his own eggs to the last. I recall the glee with which he told me how he ejected the embryo from an egg by making a small hole in one side and pouring in liquid lye, which will liquefy flesh without injury to shell.

About fifteen years ago Bob More was walking down a street in Fort Worth when he saw some bird eggs in a window. He went inside and made the acquaintance of

George E. Maxon, an amateur oologist, his junior by perhaps two decades. After procuring some eggs from him, he proposed that Maxon move to Vernon and set up a nursery business, which he agreed to back. Maxon made the move. Bob More, one deduces, wanted him for a kind of aide. That is what Maxon became, making many trips with him and often helping in the blowing, shipping and museum care of eggs. Upon finding a nest, says Maxon, "Mr. More would jump up and down like a boy, clapping his hands and calling out, 'Come here! Come here!' He might be driving like the wind on a ranch road and see a prairie chicken scoot out of the grass. He would throw on the brakes as if he were about to head into a freight train, and jump out of the car, in his excitement perhaps leaving the car in gear. He always wanted to examine the nest."

Examination might mean as much as collecting. He had, to use his own words, examined maybe a thousand kite nests without ever finding more than two eggs, often only one; yet to the last he was hopefully looking for a clutch of three. "Almost invariably," he wrote a friend, "the first set of Least Tern [in Wilbarger County] is three eggs. If the nest is broken up by predatory animals, collectors or overflow, the second set of eggs will as a rule number only two, occasionally three." It is to be regretted that he did not fully set down not only the facts established by his long and unflagging observations, but also the bird adventures he could relate with such freshness and gusto. They are to be found only in the memories of his interested friends and in his letters, usually brief, to them. His sole appearance in print seems to have been with a "List of the Birds of

Wise County, Texas," in four short installments, published in *The Naturalist*, 1894, in collaboration with J. A. Donald.

There are two kinds of bird-egg collectors. One kind merely despoils nests, either because of a puerile impulse to grasp and destroy or for mercenary reasons. This is the vandal-predator; the other kind — much rarer — cares deeply for birds and has the true scientific interest. Bob More shunned the first kind. For instance, after he had procured a few eggs from a certain individual, he learned that this man hired Mexicans to bring him eggs by the bucketful. He not only ruled out this alleged "collector" but warned friends to have no truck with him. He discouraged idle, acquisitive, notional collecting among boys, but was exceedingly interested in and helpful to a boy showing genuine interest in birds. Securing regularly, year after year, legal permits to collect bird eggs, he obeyed conservation laws as strictly as he sought to enforce them on others.

While he was waiting on Beaver Creek one fall day for a herd of cattle to come in, the first wild-goose cry of the season turned his gaze to the northern sky. It does not take either a hunter or a naturalist to thrill at that experience; Bob More was in ecstasy. "They are going to light," he exclaimed. They had not lowered their altitude or circled. "How do you know?" a friend asked. "They are signaling to each other." And presently the great wavering V-formation began to swerve and maneuver to come down.

"See that bird over there?" Bob More might say.

"Yes," a friend would answer, thinking the question an idle one.

"Know what he's doing?"

"No."

"He's calling his mate. Watch and you'll see them together very soon now."

He knew intimately the calls and ways of hundreds of birds.

His interest was too serious and deep and joyful to be called a hobby. The foremost ornithologists of America turned to him for help. In the big file of correspondence pertaining to birds and eggs that he kept segregated from business correspondence is a thick packet of letters to and from Dr. Harry C. Oberholser, lately senior biologist in the United States Department of the Interior and now curator of ornithology in the Cleveland Museum of Natural History. For nearly half a century Dr. Oberholser has been gathering data on the birds of Texas. "Your help," he wrote to More, "is indispensable for any matter that comes up regarding northwestern Texas." One of the concerns of Bob More's latter days was to secure publication of Dr. Oberholser's great work — which is truly great, no matter how viewed. He considered deeply a proposal that he ask a number of oil men for the necessary money. His judgment, however, was that oil men who made donations would regard the matter as personal and expect favors in leases or other business from the Waggoner Estate. He was unwilling to do anything that might generate prejudice toward the trust he held in keeping. The trust he always placed first in his loyalties.

The concreteness of his help to ornithologists might be illustrated by countless instances. He made various reports to Oberholser on domestic pigeons he found gone wild in New Mexico. Fresh observations were meat and drink to him, and he liked to pass them on. Details of the vast business for which he was responsible constantly held him, but one day he wrote: "I have decided to rub the bridle off and prowl around. I want to go to Santa Fe and take a Pinion Jay."

Under date of March 4, 1937, he wrote Oberholser:

I am shipping you the two pigeon eggs. They were found dried up, and the contents in hard form are now inside the eggs. I am afraid that the shaking up they will get will break through the shell.

I have not, as yet, found time to check up the breeding dates on the Great Horned Owl, but will try to get down to it and give you the information. I have taken three sets of Great Horned Owl, that is, the Western, this spring; the first on February 22, and two sets a day or two later. Yesterday, I examined a nest with one infertile egg, and one bird about a day old. This nest also contained the remnants of a cottontail rabbit and two starlings.

1937 will complete my fiftieth year with the birds. I guess I have examined hundreds of the Great Horned Owl nests, and with the exception of the one nest which contained parts of a broken-wing duck and the nest I saw yesterday, I have never found as much as a feather in them, except, of course, the mother bird's breast feathers, with which she lines her nest. In all other nests, the food supply was always rodents.

If I can give you any further information, please call on me, and incidentally, if you would like, I will mail you a copy of my duplicate list and be glad to give you anything therein that you might need or care for.

In another letter to Oberholser, three years later, he bubbled forth: "I do not know whether I told you or not, but about six weeks ago I took a set of twelve Lesser Prairie Hen's eggs, the first I ever saw." He had been looking for a nest of this now rare bird for thirty years. He found it in Wheeler County, Texas. "The set of eggs," he goes on, "was perfectly nice, about five or six days incubated. Also, I saw nineteen males doing their booming, about three hundred yards away. They were certainly putting on a show right in the short grass in the open prairie. They paid no attention to us in a car. One came within twenty feet of us."

Any real naturalist is a conservationist. The Mississippi kite, of which great numbers have in recent years come to make their home on the Waggoner Ranch, was Bob More's favorite bird. Extracts from two letters that he wrote J. C. Braly, of Portland, Oregon, will reveal something of his attitude not only toward this bird but toward birds in general.

September 22, 1928: I learned something this year about the Kite. I figured that if I let the birds lay and then collected the eggs, I would later find an occasional pair I had overlooked raising their young. I was figuring on taking the parents and the young.

As much as I know of these birds, and as closely as I have watched them for the last twenty-eight years, they sure fooled me. The old bird does not stay around the nest after the eggs are hatched. I have sat for an hour at a time and neither one of them would come around. In addition to that, after the young leave the nest, you cannot get within two hundred or three hundred yards of either of them. So, next year, I will have to take you what you want while the eggs are in the nest. I hate to kill them, hate to kill anything, but I have promised you and Jewett a pair of these birds, each, and I will sure get them for you.

July 2, 1930: I was back in the pasture on June 22nd, drove up to one of the chuck wagons and about forty feet away these three birds (No. 329 — Mississippi Kites) and two White Neck Ravens were hanging on limbs. They had evidently been killed several hours. I asked the cook what his idea was for killing the Hawks, and he said they ate up the chickens. I skinned those three as good as I could, dissected them and showed that cook that everything in each bird's stomach was grasshoppers, beetles and crawfish. I do not believe he will ever kill any more Mississippi Kites. If you can use the skins, I am only too glad for you to get them.

In general, Bob More was for letting nature balance itself. An occasional roadrunner might sometimes eat a young quail, but he recognized the roadrunner as predominantly beneficial both to the land it lives on and the wildlife dependent on that land. In conservation he was not guided by sentiment alone. He agreed with W. T. Waggoner that a quail or a wild turkey will soon eat its own weight in insects. "Birds are man's best friends," he often said. "If they were suddenly destroyed, insects would within a short time destroy the vegetation on which the human race is dependent."

His ambition for many years was to have a tank on every section of the Waggoner lands and, by light stocking, to bring the grasses back to pristine lushness. This would be fine for the cattle, for the benefit of which water and grass are supposed to exist. It would be superb for birds also, and nothing pleased Bob More better than the vast increase, in both species and numbers, of land and water birds which resulted from his policy. In the end he regarded the Waggoner Ranch — placed by nature along Beaver Creek and the Wichita River, further watered by extensive impoundments, its restored grasses added to in places by cultivated grains — as the greatest bird preserve in Texas. His standing order to harvesters was to leave a patch of grain around every wild-turkey nest discovered in a field. He estimated the number of wild turkeys on the Waggoner land at more than three thousand. He had to accept the fact that oil-well crews prove inimical to game birds in areas they make uncontrollable, but he had the satisfaction of knowing that his ranch hands came to exercise a protective friendship for birds, whether game or not.

He could look with a shrewd eye at tractors plowing the fields, and at the same time exult in the sight of gulls and ravens grabbing worms from the turned-up soil. He directed blitzkrieg-looking bulldozers uprooting pastures of mesquite to make room for grass, but also he saw with elation the darting of kites and scissortails above the trees in which they make their home. After all the clearing was over, there would be plenty of mesquites left for their nests.

In 1937, when Herbert Brandt — man of affairs, one of the leading ornithologists of America, and spirit of the Bird Research Foundation of Cleveland, Ohio, which is associated with the Cleveland Museum of Natural History — made his fourth trip to Texas, he was the guest of Bob More. During the succeeding years he was Bob More's intimate in ornithological matters, and the two became very dear friends. About a third of *Bird Adventures in Texas,* which Herbert Brandt brought out in 1940, is devoted to observations made under the guidance of Bob More on the Waggoner Ranch. This section contains a good account of the More collection, and the book itself is dedicated to him.

Learning of the proposed dedication, before the book was published, Bob More wrote Brandt in this characteristic vein: "You know the government does not put a man's picture on stamps as long as he is living. If he stays good until he dies, he is good afterwards and you never can tell. Anyhow, you might not be making a mistake when you omitted the dedication. I can appreciate your feelings in the matter, but maybe it was just feelings with you."

In 1939 Bob More sent Brandt his mounted California condor — "because it wasn't being cared for" in his own museum. "Do not write back and thank me," he enjoined. "You have already done that." According to Brandt, the specimen arrived "in perfect condition" and went on exhibition immediately in the Cleveland Museum of Natural History.

In March, 1941 — only six months before their friend died — some oil men in Wichita Falls, under the leadership of John L. McMahon, arranged a surprise party for Bob More, to show how much they liked and appreciated him. They wanted to give him a present. At first they thought of a gold watch; but, as R. B. Anderson pointed out to one of them, Bob More had had two or three gold watches but always preferred an Ingersoll. A gun? He had guns that he rarely used. There was only one thing to give that would be precious to him. They turned to Herbert Brandt. His letter concluding the negotiations expresses much:

We are shipping this day, via Prepaid Express, insured for $600, a box of eight sets of the rarest of North American birds' eggs. None of these, I believe, are represented in the More collection. They were taken by the writer personally, during his Alaska expedition of 1924. In order to reach Hooper Bay, we mushed in with dog teams for some 850 miles, requiring about a hundred dogs, and 40 days of storm-beset Arctic travel.

You may well imagine that with the fine collection Bob More has amassed, it is extremely difficult to supply him with any new species. So, in order to add the proper romance and interest to your dinner in his honor, it was necessary for me to draw on the very best material that I could find on two continents. Therefore, I am sending you a great Andean Condor, the result of my expedition to Chile in 1935. This bird was captured in co-operation with Carlos Reed, the head of the Zoological Gardens of Santiago, and grandson of the Doctor Reed who was physician on board *The Beagle* when Darwin made his famous trip through the Humboldt Current and laid the foundation for his theory on evolution.

Of the birds' eggs you will note that among them are sets of the Emperor Goose and Cackling Goose, two of the rarest and most beautiful of the geese; also three sets of the rare Arctic Eiders, and two sets of the most beautiful of all shorebirds' eggs as well as among the least known — the Pectoral Sandpiper, and the Ruddy Turnstone. Bob knows how few American Scoter's eggs there are in collections.

I hope that you have as much fun and as many thrills at your party, presenting them to Bob, as I had in collecting them. I always maintained that I would never part with any of these personally taken rarities, but in all my wide world there is not a finer man than Bob More, nor is there any other naturalist to whom I would pass them on.

Two or three weeks after the party, Bob More wrote Brandt:

Now, to start with, I know I am just as rotten as a fellow could be. I owe you three letters and a thousand thanks for the eggs and the Andean Condor. I have many reasons why

I have overlooked writing, but am like the fellow that was asked to have a drink and said there were a thousand good reasons why he should not take it but he could not think of a one of them.

Those boys really put on a show . . . Now that spring is here, I wish you would bundle up your whole bunch and come on down. I will go with you anywhere except on the ocean. The birds on the coast should be in full bloom by the time you get here. I have taken turkey eggs several seasons by the 24th of April and some of them were incubated. We could make a trip to Mexico or the Big Bend. Anywhere you want to go and anything you want to do . . . If you would like to take a set of Attwater's Prairie Chicken, a pair of the birds and the eggs, we will go to the King Ranch and get them. They should be nesting now. A man on the King Ranch superintending the cleaning off of brush told me he would spot the nests for me any time I would let him know. This is a rare chance.

Now don't do like I have done. Go ahead and let me hear from you. I am still thanking you for the eggs and Condor. I am sending you a color moving picture film of the Waggoner turkeys taken by Trapper Davis. He has almost completed another roll of the different birds he ran into down there. He started the roll off with the Red Bird. As soon as it is completed and developed, I will send it.

It is a rare, wonderful, delightful and blessed thing for a man to carry with him until he goes over the hill at the end of a long road the interest in some good and gracious subject acquired when the dew of morning was still in his eyes — an interest that all through the years has made the whole world more interesting for him, given him joy and solace, and meant refreshment and enrichment of life to others as well as to himself.

To many people — and with reason — Bob More will

be remembered as the manager of the Waggoner Estate. He was, emphatically, an extraordinarily capable businessman, a master of prosperity. Keeping his trust with others, he also built up a fortune of his own. He was a man of the world, but he was not worldly. His "immortal residue" lies not in acres, cows, or oil. It lies in the visible and enlightening proof of a lifetime of enthusiasm, intelligence and civilized sympathy for nature, as evidenced in the oological collection surviving him. It and it alone, in the long run, will be his monument. He often expressed the wish that it be kept intact. The idea that it or any part of it should ever be sold was intolerable to him.

Although the whole man went afield when Bob More was with the birds, something remains to be said of his characteristics. He was five feet, seven and one-half inches tall and weighed between 130 and 135 pounds. He was made out of wire, muscle and nerves. He lived in a hurry, worked in a hurry and died in a hurry, breathing less than two hours after his heart failed him in his office. Five or six hours of sleep at night were enough for him. He often went to his office after supper and stayed until midnight — frequently blowing eggs in these quiet hours. Egg blowing was something he couldn't rush without making the holes too big. "The only time I have to myself is between midnight and four o'clock in the morning," he would explain, "and the cowboys wake me up then." It is claimed that he could write a telegram, listen to a report and talk over the telephone all at one time.

In spite of all the affairs he tended to, and the cares that beset him from boyhood — cares that few people knew about — he often seemed a happy-go-lucky sort of fellow. He had the faculty of dismissing troubles when they were out of season. Getting behind with a huge stack of correspondence did not worry him. "Most letters answer themselves in sixty days," he observed.

Wherever he was, whatever he was doing, no matter how much he was enjoying the present, his energy was leaping ahead. To use his own expression, he lived "as busy as triplets." He sometimes drove for forty-eight hours at a stretch. It was no uncommon thing for him, with someone to relieve him at the wheel, to drive the 420 miles from Vernon to the headquarters of the Waggoner ranch in New Mexico, race around some on the ranch itself, go out of the way to inspect an irrigated farm of his own, and return to Vernon — all within a day and night. He had the halfway point on this often-made drive located by a certain telephone pole. On the way to New Mexico, George Maxon says, his mind would be working with what lay ahead of him until he reached that pole; then as he raced on, it would begin to concern itself with what lay behind, to which he would soon be returning. Going back east, about the time he passed that halfway point he would begin to figure on the next trip to New Mexico. On trips like this — and they were the usual kind with him — he often stopped only long enough to buy a hamburger to eat in the car. If he paused for a meal, he could consume it and write a postcard in five minutes. He was a light eater, but ate with gusto what he did eat.

It was Go, Go, Go. But if somebody warned him against excessive speeding, he airily replied, "The Lord's got both arms around me." Good cars were his one extravagance — if they were an extravagance, considering the uses he made of them. He generally traded in for a new one every three or four months. He didn't need roads, but could drive "about anywhere a drag rope could go." He never took to airplanes.

He wore old clothes and had no use for vest or overcoat. He rolled his own cigarettes in old-fashioned brown papers. He was strongly averse to publicity, and distrusted all "publicity hounds." A scrapbook, which he kept in a very desultory manner, contains various pictures of ranchmen and ranch scenes, a photograph of Will Rogers and Charles M. Russell together, a print of a Russell picture — but not even a snapshot of himself.

He had read the Bible entirely through more than once and was always ready with scriptural citations. He kept up with the world through newspapers and magazines, and knew his books and journals on ornithology and oology. Now and then he had time for a book on frontier or ranch life. His life was too crowded, though, to allow for much leisurely reading. Even on the subject of birds, he was more interested in firsthand observations than in printed words.

He liked people — many people and many kinds of people. He had a going-out way to people he liked. He loved to talk, and on a genial subject to a congenial listener his talk was like the welling up of an inexhaustible fresh spring of water. He had a tenacious and exact memory — a part of his mental discipline against guesses and loose knowledge; and when he brought up incident or character out of memory's storehouse, the fire of his energy, tempered by humor and humanity, lit the subject up like lightning at night illuminating the crests of clouds.

He made judgments just as he talked — from impulse,

backed by knowledge and experience. "He wasn't the think-it-over type," summed up his good friend Tony Hazelwood, the Waggoner range foreman. "You could ask him a question and you'd have an answer in a second. It was *yes* or it was *no*." When Mrs. Ruth Riall became his office secretary in 1936, he said to her, "There are just three words in the English language: *Hell* and *Yes* and *No*, Hell, yes, and Hell, no. If you know how to say these words and know when to say them, you can use mud for brains." One of the things that pleased him toward the end of his life was a nameplate for his desk, presented by R. B. Anderson. The plate is three-sided and revolves. One side, which he kept showing most of the time, reads, "R. L. More." The second side reads, "Hell, Yes," and the third side, "Hell, No."

He had many original expressions. When he left the office, he would say, to quote Mrs. Riall, "Run this place like I want you to. I'm going out to set the world on fire." Or, he might say, "Run this place the way you want to; I'm going down here about forty miles to shut a gate." Again, his parting words would be, "If anybody wants me, tell them I've gone to the wild bunch."

If he got a new idea about anything, he would bubble out to an intimate, "I'm just as smart as the devil." If somebody did something for him that he liked, he would say, "I wouldn't trade you for the best mule in Wilbarger County." On the other hand, praise concerning him was likely to be countered with some such self-deprecation as, "Now, he's making a fuss over me with both hands."

To individuals who wanted him to let down the bars, especially regarding the Waggoner interests, he would reply, "That would be taking the bridle off." One of his maxims was, "If anything suggests that a move is wrong, don't make it." Expressive of his canniness he would say, "I'm just like a rabbit. Trust nothing. It might be a dog." Again, "People put words in my mouth. So don't take my word. Get my signature." Yet again, "Don't do anything you can't swear to. You'll hobble yourself in short grass."

He didn't mind the reputation of being hard-boiled — which he probably was, in business matters. One man to whom Tom Waggoner had sold certain oil-drilling rights got a dry hole that broke him. He argued that he should have his money back. "All right," Tom Waggoner agreed, "if Bob More says so." Bob More just laughed, as Waggoner knew he would. Another operator, after dickering on a lease, finally signed the contract as the Waggoner manager had dictated it. Then he left town for a remote field of operations. Three days later, as the story goes, a cowboy found him away out forty miles from nowhere, on a dim road, his car stuck in quicksand. "Gracious," the cowboy said, "you must be getting pretty hungry by now."

"No, no," the operator replied, "I've got one of Bob More's contracts with me and it has enough provisions to last any man through any famine."

"I never gave any man credit for anything in my life," Bob More would say, meaning that he never bragged on an employee; but he did. One evening he drove into Austin at dark with his agent, Dwight Parnell, to fight an oil company before the Railroad Commission on the morrow. It took a stenographer all night and until ten o'clock next morning to write the brief as dictated. Her work appeared to be perfect. Bob More reached into his pocket and pulled out a fifty-dollar bill in payment; the young lady was almost stunned. He was tolerant in judgments of men, encouraging with words, and charitable with money. His material help to the needy was steady and abounding, but he always wanted it kept secret. When approached annually by the Red Cross for a contribution, which was not niggardly, he would say, while signing a check, "You know the rules." (No publicity.)

Although the manager of a great ranch, an excellent judge of cattle — yet perhaps a better judge of men who actually did the work with cattle — and a trader in large numbers of livestock, he mounted a horse, it is said, only two times in the last fifty-six years of his life. He was a superb executive in picking captains and superintendents.

If he worked hard, he worked freely. He had a fine zest for what he was doing, though occasionally he came to the conclusion that "this life is all bug dust." Along with work, nature and people, he liked jokes; but his sense of humor seemed to me better expressed in incisive anecdotes, revealing human character, than in jokes for the jokes' sake. I'm not sure if he always knew, and certainly others sometimes did not know, just when he was joking. On my last visit to him, I remarked, while he followed me to the stairway, that I had a bedroll and a coffeepot in my car so that I could camp wherever I wanted to out in New Mexico. "Here, take this," he said with a quick gesture, as he reached up and got a hair rope from a buck's antlers on the wall. "It will keep the rattlesnakes off you at night. That's what it was made for."

"That's just an old belief that's been exploded," I said.

"No. You don't see insects crawling over a hair rope. Honestly. Take it, take it, and be sure to string it around your pallet when you bed down on the ground."

I don't know if Bob More seriously believed in the efficacy of horsehair ropes against crawling rattlesnakes or not. Was he finding an excuse to give me a remembrance? Anyhow, he seemed to care for my welfare, and I went on down the stairs and out on the street with a glad heart. As I went, I was thinking how someday I would come back and get more of his stories about Jimmie Roberts and persuade him to tell me something for an article on himself. That five weeks later his articulate vitality would have become inanimation locked in perpetual silence no more occurred to me than the pregnability of Gibraltar seemed possible to the Prudential Life Insurance Company only a short time before. Anyway, he packed and crammed sixty-eight years — lacking only ten days — with life without ever growing old. Those whom the gods love die young at whatever age.

Bob More was a man of sentiment though never sentimental. He had a nostalgia for the past as well as love for friends. In his offices, along with pictures of the Waggoner men, Will Rogers and other friends, he had assembled ox yokes, horns of the old-time Texas steer, coffee mills, cowbells, branding irons, spurs and many other artifacts expressive of the pioneer life he was born to. One can imagine him sometimes, riding in the night, recalling the Indian stories that his mother used to tell at bedtime.

His magnetism was expressed in his voice and energetic look. "You have the peculiar property in your voice, Bob," Herbert Brandt wrote him, "that gives a fellow encouragement to do things." Yet he took no active part in social or civic movements. Despite his many associations and his liking for people, he was not a joiner. He did belong to the Masonic Order. He was, above all, an individual. His refusal to kill a certain rattlesnake that let him alone while he stood almost over it, unseeing, was just one of many quirks of conduct and philosophy that marked him as "a little queer" — delightfully queer. I can imagine him chuckling with warm sympathy at the words of his cherished Charles M. Russell: "I am old-fashioned and peculiar in my dress. I am eccentric (that is a polite way of saying you are crazy). I believe in luck and have had lots of it . . . Any time I cash in now, I win."

Not that there was anything outlandish about Bob More's individualism. He had the common touch to a high degree. A queer thing to me is that while making a fortune for himself, and adding to the Waggoner millions, he seemed to care nothing for money in itself. He did not waste it; no doubt he enjoyed making it, and he understood how to some people it is the be-all and the end-all of life, but it wasn't so for a minute to him. With all his geniality, winsomeness and eagerness, he kept something of his essential soul back, apart, in serene reserve. What was there behind this man who, after having weighed out the last of a long string of Herefords and having carelessly pocketed a quarter-million-dollar check — for the Waggoner Estate — yelled like a boy, "Let's go shoot a frog"?

Sometimes, I am sure, this man was more lonely than other people knew. Pipelines, oil fields, oil wells, oil companies, oil operators, oil refineries, filling stations, railroads, tractors, fleets of trucks, herds, granaries, colonies of farmers, income taxes, payrolls — "four millionaires and a white woman," as he would jocularly say, "on my hands." Go, go, go; sign, sign, sign; people, people, people. But over there, just to one side, that quiet nest of the quiet-voiced bluebird, with five eggs in it, as lovely in shape as in their azure tinting.

I did not know Bob More as well as I loved him. On each of the few occasions that I talked with him, beginning in 1931, I left hungry for further association. He made an immense appeal to my imagination as well as to my feelings of friendship. I have written the essay to express a debt of honor that I feel owing to a magnanimous nature, an interesting and vivid character, and a contributor to civilization on the soil into which his roots went deep.

Ed Bateman, Wildcatter

A WILDCATTER is a person who drills for oil in a place oil is not known to exist. Bankers consider his business about as safe as buying lottery tickets.

According to oil-field tradition, the original wildcatters drilled so far from town and all proven territory that they used hoot owls for chickens and wildcats for watchdogs; hence the name.

In 1930, Ed Bateman, a Texas wildcatter, brought in the biggest discovery well in the history of the oil industry. He sold out the lease block on which the well was located and divided his portion of the money two ways — half for a family trust fund to buy a ranch, and half for more wildcatting. The wildcatting portion soon vanished into the ground without visible returns. In 1933 he and his family settled on the ranch, and Ed Bateman became a part of the harmony characterized by mesquite bushes, jackrabbits, coyotes and his own quarter horses. Then in 1943 an oil company to which he had leased the ranch brought in a well. Today, the ranch contains an oil field with thirty-nine producing wells.

"The Bateman luck" is a common phrase among oil people and ranch people scattered over Texas. Ed Bateman can well say, "I believe in luck. I've had lots of it."

But there's more to the business than that — a very great deal more. We'll have to backtrack. Fifty-five years ago, away down on the Suwannee River in Georgia, Ed Bateman was born to an educated minister and his educated wife. When Ed was a mere boy, his father died. Ed helped his mother educate his sisters. Books in the home and educated family friends contributed perhaps more to his education than the scanty schooling he received.

At eighteen he came to Texas. Before the United States entered World War I he was a newspaper reporter. He was designated as a combat correspondent, but something happened, somewhere, behind the curtain of chance, and he did not get across. In 1915 he married, and from that date to this it has been "we" with Caroline and Ed Bateman. They have reared two children. In 1919 the oil business came to Texas with postwar boom, frenzy, fury, fortune, and failure. Ed Bateman reported oil activities. He crisscrossed Texas, went into Arkansas, Louisiana, Oklahoma.

In the rushing days of the early twenties, while America was arriving at the oil-consuming automobile age, "nobody knew how to write about oil," Ed Bateman says. "Everybody in the business was learning from everybody else." He himself was learning a lot more than the chronicling of dry holes, gushers, boom towns, lease-hound oracles and federal prosecution of bogus promoters required. He read geology. He learned to read the underground sign inherent in well cuttings and cores. He had a chance to meet nearly everybody who was playing a game. He knew enough to ask questions that would draw out enlightening answers.

In 1925 he decided to quit newspapering and "shoot for the moon." He started in as a lease hound, buying and selling leases. "Some people made fortunes out of the leases I sold them," he says. He switched to digging wells himself.

"The only way to find oil," he says, "is to put down a hole. Shooting for the moon means putting up everything you've got on the chance. It's all or nothing. But a wildcatter does not have to make a strike with his first well in order to keep on getting backing. Well after well can be as dry as a front seat in hell, but if the wildcatter is sincere, honest and capable, he can get backing for another hole. He has to keep on drilling, keep on hoping and believing, keep on selling hope and belief. In the end, of course, Lady Luck must be on his side. Lady Luck and the Law of Probabilities work together. The capable wildcatter studies the Law of Probabilities."

Some wildcatters hire drillers with rigs; some don't. Ed Bateman had his own equipment, hired his own crew — the roughnecks. For about two years he was one of them, working on the rig itself, largely to learn the whole technique of drilling and to be able to direct every movement in drilling operations.

He drilled east and he drilled west. In six years' time he put down forty-one holes, one after the other — in Texas, Oklahoma and Louisiana — without drawing up a bucket of oil. "Wildcatting is a cruel business," he says. "It is a tooth-and-claw business. Mother Nature does not like to be gutted, and gutting her is what the driller is doing. She resists. The oil hunters are clannish. They know that a man without experience can't find oil, but they are open-natured to their own kind. I was a trained questioner, and as I drilled, I learned from others as well as from experience. We burned, we froze, we starved, we sweated. Once, west of the Pecos, I was neighbor to another wildcatter who ran out of absolutely everything but determination. The only fuel that he could afford for the steam boiler which powered his engine was sotol stalks from the barren range around him. You know, sotol is enough like a yucca that one of its names is saw yucca; sotol stalks are about as substantial as wisps of hay. I wanted to back that fellow with money, but I didn't have any. I loaned him parts of drilling machinery. We belonged to the same fraternity; the ties in that fraternity go deep."

The first step in getting backing for a wildcat well is to lease a certain amount of acreage, perhaps for a dollar or so an acre, perhaps by merely guaranteeing a test well to the owner of the land. In either case the owner, according to standard lease forms, gets a one-eighth royalty — one barrel out of every eight produced on his land, free of all cost to him. Having leased a block of land and "spudded-in" (started drilling) a well, or else having obligated himself to spud-in by a certain date, the independent operator sells chances on his success. He subleases, for cash, parts of the land he controls. The principal buyers are major oil companies; next come independent companies and individuals, including other wildcatters. It is a common practice for wildcatters who are sufficiently ahead in the game to swap leases with each other. The buyer of a lease from a wildcatter usually spreads his acreage; if he buys forty acres, he will bracket the well from four sides with four ten-acre tracts. By selling chances on there being "sand" — oil-bearing sand — at the bottom of the hole he is drilling, the wildcatter may realize enough money to pay the cost of drilling, even if the hole turns out dry. Sometimes the drilling crew will work for nothing but beans and bacon and the promise of shares in the expected oil.

The king of all the wildcatters operating in Texas and adjacent territory was the late Colonel A. E. Humphreys. He used to say, "We must leave tracks" — his version of Longfellow's "footprints on the sands of time." Gold is not the only thing that occurs where you find it. Oil is where you find it. If a wildcatter makes enough tracks deep enough over enough country, the Law of Chance, or of Probabilities, is with him. The wildcatter does the exploring; the big oil companies, according to established policy, buy chances on his luck, pluck and whatever else he has.

According to policy, I said. In 1930 no oil company extended its policy to Dad Joiner, who was drilling on a shoestring in Rusk County of east Texas. He had already put down two dry holes in the vicinity. Not even another wildcatter had acreage with him, though the wildcatters were watching him. Only the backing of local residents kept him going. In September, 1930, at a depth of 3,536 feet, he hit the oil-bearing Woodbine sand, but his finances were so exhausted that he had to make a deal with an independent operator to case the well. It was a small producer. Informed geologists said he was in a local sand. The big operators were not interested. Depression was already constricting the nation and the world. Crude oil that had been $3.50 a barrel ten years back was on the way to go begging at ten cents a barrel. As subsequent exploration demonstrated, had Dad Joiner sunk his well a thousand feet east of his location, it would have proved dry. Nobody in 1930 suspected that he had brought in the discovery well on the extreme eastern and southern point of what was to be proven the greatest oil field in the world.

One of the wildcatters watching was Ed Bateman. He was convinced. He obtained a lease on 1,488 acres of land owned by the Crim family, near the village of Kilgore, about fifteen miles north of Dad Joiner's well. He needed cash to drill. Not a major oil company or an established independent would buy an acre of his lease; only individual lease buyers joined him. The big boys wished him well, but told him that he might as well fish for bass in an alkali flat as bore for oil in that location. The big companies had "shot" all over the territory with their geophysical instruments and found absolutely no indication of an oil trap's existence. The Ed Bateman well kept on going down.

It is the law in Texas — and in other states — that every driller of an oil well must identify strata by the cuttings and cores of earth through which he bores, log them, and file his log with the state — for public information. The logs of a number of wells drilled over any particular region give a profile map of its subsurface formations that is as clear as a contour map of its surface. Any informed driller reads logs. After he has read enough of them, he knows what he is coming to as well as a horseman riding down a hillside knows what's ahead of him. Ed Bateman knew how to read signs deep down.

On the morning of December 19, 1930, he had reason to believe that his drill stem would that day penetrate the Woodbine sand. A lot of people were out at the well, standing back, waiting. He had ordered a special core head from Houston to drill through a quartzite sandcap. It took an hour to cut through it. Then the drill stem went on down twelve feet. The crew pulled out a core.

Ed Bateman looked at the cylinder-shaped sample of earthen matter, smelled it, took a bit of it on the end of his finger, walked over to the car in which his wife Caroline was sitting and put his finger near enough her nose for a sniff. Without saying a word, he walked back to the derrick floor.

Onlookers, many of them keen on oil-well techniques, rushed to the car. "What did he say?" "What did he say?" they asked.

"He did not say anything," Mrs. Bateman answered. The essential fact could not be kept back long. The twelve-foot core was of Woodbine sand heavily impregnated with oil. Oil does not occur in underground lakes and streams like water. It is exceedingly volatile and is found compressed in the pores of such firm strata as sandstone and lime, making possible such a core as came to the surface that day. The Bateman well was only 3,642 feet deep, a depth now regarded as shallow. It had to be cased. Casing was rushed out and put down. Then the test came.

In thirty-eight minutes the well flowed 917 barrels of oil into a thousand-barrel tank that had been hastily set up. It was capable of gushing out 36,000 barrels of oil a day. It still holds the record for being, in volume of production, the biggest wildcat discovery well ever drilled. It still produces by flowing, and according to a recent test has a potential of 2,500 barrels a day. Only proration and other controls based on science have kept it and thousands of other wells in the East Texas Oil Field from being ruined by salt water, which pressures beneath nearly all oil beds, trying to get up.

Within a few weeks after this historic well was brought in, the Moncrief-Farrell well, fifteen miles on north, hit the Woodbine sand and gushed. The Dad Joiner, Ed Bateman and Moncrief-Farrell drills had punctured a stratigraphic trap, the sealed-off sands of which were saturated with five billion barrels of oil. Some 30,000 producing wells have been sunk into the 128,000 acres of this oil trap — a strip of inconceivably ancient shore-line about forty-five miles long and from five to seven miles wide — in which geological forces bottled the oil and held it until wildcatters bored down and un-corked it.

Ed Bateman did not want to produce, much less refine, oil. He wanted to hunt — wildcat — for it and find it. Also, he "knew all along" that someday he was going to own a parcel of the vast expanse of land that is Texas. Within less than a month he sold out his well and the lease block on which many other producing wells were to be sunk. What he got for his portion was not chicken feed. Half of the proceeds, as I have already told, he put into a trust fund in his wife's name. The trust bought a ranch of 25,000 acres in King County in western Texas.

A wildcatter wants money for more wildcats. Ed Bateman was not set in his ways of wildcatting with the half-fortune designated for that purpose. He wildcatted for gold mines in the Sierra Madre of northern Mexico. He sent an expedition to Cuba to hunt oil. He prospected for oil in Canada and California. He did not find gold. He did not bring in another discovery well. When he moved to the ranch with his family in 1933, he was con-tent to be there. He did not know cattle, but he had known horses from boyhood. He began specializing in quarter horses, as an aside from steer raising, and now the Bateman horses are adding to his name.

Contented with being a ranchman, he's still a wildcatter. He thinks the country needs wildcatter spirit and enterprise now as never before. Oil is still where you find it, and not enough of it is being found to supply increasing demands.

The popular idea is that exploring for oil in these scientific times is confined to surface surveys with seismographs and gravity meters. All any instrument can reveal is subsurface formations favorable to oil. Such a formation, or trap, does not necessarily hold oil; not all jugs hold whiskey. No instrument reveals oil itself any more than a peach switch reveals hidden gold. And a lot of oil has been found that was not in formations indicated by instruments. The structures pertaining to the biggest underground reserve of oil ever tapped and exploited — the East Texas Oil Field — did not say and still do not say a thing to any instrument. The only certain way to find out if oil is underground is to drill for it.

"Despite all to the contrary," Ed Bateman says, "the wildcatters are the true discoverers in the search for oil. In the aggregate, they have drilled far more wells than all the big companies combined — always in the strangest sorts of places. They have been short on science but long on practical knowledge and willingness to play the game with Lady Luck.

"It is attractive and profitable for big companies to exploit oil in the Middle East; it is not necessary for the economy of America. Income taxes are far more favorable to producers of oil than to its discoverers. All sorts of federal rules hem the wildcatter in. The wildcatter can't function by rule.

"There are just as many chances for wildcatters in the Western Hemisphere as there ever were. Machinery is ready now to drill wells four miles deep. The time can come when men will drill wells ten miles deep, down to the granite core of the earth, to find stores of oil or other energy in traps not yet suspected. There's plenty of undiscovered oil this side of such depths.

"The wildcatter does not have to start out with a fortune. He'll do better if he's close to broke. He'll have to keep costs down, and that will put him on the fringes. On the fringes and beyond are where new discoveries are to be made. What if the wildcatter does suffer? When you buck Nature, you are going to suffer a lot. Security by either the government route or the corporation route may be all right for some people. Security is not what Columbus and the Curies were after. Security is not what the wildcatter is after. Whether he hits the pay or not, he gets a solid satisfaction, a kind of spiritual experience, in piercing the unknown and finding an answer that to him is personal."

Ed Bateman swears that when the Bateman Trust Estate bought that ranch of 25,000 acres he had no knowledge of oil under it. Of course, he thought that oil might be under it; he thinks that oil might be under any land not proven barren. When, as trustee, he oil-leased the ranch to a big company, he inserted a proviso calling for one test well by a certain date. The company did not make any subsurface survey with instruments; it just made a location. When a producer came in, the Batemans, following west Texas tradition, presented every member of the crew with a pair of shop-made boots. The company drillers went on putting down more wells, defining and developing the field. They found that had they set their first well between three and four hundred yards off in a certain direction from where they did set it, the hole would have been a dry one. In that case, another well would not have been drilled. The field peters out near a fence line dividing the Bateman ranch from a neighbor's. Lady Luck was around.

"No," Ed Bateman says, "I certainly didn't buy the ranch for more oil. If it did not have a drop of oil, I would not trade it for the biggest oil company in the world. If I had that company I'd have to run it. I've never wanted money for the sake of wealth, only for what money will buy — including wildcat chances. I've wanted a rounded life."

Ed Bateman is a philosopher. There are many things in his philosophy that many oil men have never dreamed of. Sometimes the old urge to write seizes him. I have a rare little book that he not only wrote but designed and set with his own hands. One sketch in it is about a hermit philosopher-geologist who claimed to know the secret of finding "enough petroleum to endow this planet for ages." Last year Bateman published at his own expense a brief book entitled *Horse Breaker*. It has some observations new to print.

Ed Bateman likes to see the coyotes free on the range and sometimes to hunt them with hounds. If one starts stealing his turkeys or chickens, he shoots at it and it generally takes the hint. He likes to hear the long, long coyote wail in the night and the concerted coyote singing. He likes to sit on the ranch gallery when the wind is coming soft from the south and have long, long thoughts. In some respects, wildcatting is a synonym for imagination as well as for daring.

A Cowboy Preacher and His Book

O NE of the most disgusting counterfeits of the cowboy is that class of young preachers who covet the
appellation. What one is to understand by the term
"cowboy preacher" I have never yet learned. If it means
a man who has been a cowboy, and, having quit the
cattle business, has gone into the ministry, then the term
"cowboy preacher" has in many instances been decidedly
misapplied.

It is amusing to see a little six-bit fellow start out to
slinging slang from the pulpit, posing as a cowboy preacher.
He usually procures a ten-ounce hat with a leather band and
a pair of high-heeled boots, and then he is riding. I met one
such, and in conversation with him found, to my astonish-
ment and disgust, that he had never been on a regular cow
ranch in his life. His experience consisted, I am convinced,
of sitting on the fence and seeing the herd go by, or watching his mother milk an East Texas dogie cow. He didn't
know the first letter in the cowman's alphabet.

The quotation is from the autobiography of an old-
time cowhand named James who had himself turned
preacher. For more than half a century the American
people have been hearing about cowboy preachers,

cowboy professors, cowboy humorists, cowboy mayors, cowboy bankers, and the like. Some of the men so designated have been real cowboys; a lot of them haven't. The number of range hands who toward the close of the last century and in the opening years of this century became preachers was considerable. Two of them, both Texans, wrote genuine books about range life. The lesser known is J. W. Anderson's *From the Plains to the Pulpit,* published in Houston in 1907.

The other book, *Cowboy Life in Texas, or 27 Years a Maverick,* by W. S. James, 1903, was printed by a Chicago firm for distribution by butcher boys on trains. Someday somebody will give the train butchers of an epoch now about passed away due credit as literary purveyors to the American public. Only secondhand book dealers can now purvey *Cowboy Life in Texas, or 27 Years a Maverick.* Like Anderson's *From the Plains to the Pulpit* and many another good chronicle of the past, it is out of print.

W. S. James is not to be confused with the present-day cowboy writer named Will James, who in one of his books, *Lone Cowboy,* seems proud of having been a horse thief. I prefer the old Texas preacher's autobiography to Will James's. It is more sincere and natural. I'm writing about his cowboy-preacher book partly in the hope of learning something. According to his own record, he was born in Tarrant County in 1857. Everything he says shows that he had "laid out with the dry cattle" many a night. He was converted in 1885 and began working "as a missionary, not a minister," among ranch people. He also kept on working as a cowhand.

A single quotation will show that he got the right words and the right tune, both, into his style. He says:

I remember a story told on an old vinegaroon preacher, one of those old fellows who branded mavericks during the week, or hired it done, and preached on Sunday to pay for it. As some of the boys put it, he had to do something to square accounts with the Lord. He was a great stickler for water. One Sunday while preaching on the subject of baptism he related what some Methodist brother had to say about the work of John the Baptist at Jordan. He became very much exercised over it. The brother had said that maybe John had a long-handled dipper with which he dipped the water out of Jordan and poured it on the people. The old preacher called out in stentorian tones (and he had a voice like a Spanish burro), "How long was that dipper handle?" After a pause, "How long was that dipper handle?" After a longer pause, in louder tones than before he called out again, "How long was that dipper handle, I say?" An old lady of the Methodist persuasion arose to her feet and pointing her fat, chubby finger at the preacher said: "About as long as your branding iron handle you branded my calves with, parson."

The old fellow stood rooted to the spot for the moment and then said: "Let us pray." He was a jolly old fellow and often told the story on himself. Whether it was true or not I cannot say.

James has several pages, illustrated by anecdotes, on cowboy lingo. The naming of horses, he says, "was as a rule accidental. One time a new horse let fly and kicked at one of the boys. He went by the name of Heels until he passed in his chips. Another horse we had that was mean to kick never had any name but Dirty Heels. A little colt of fine blood that was left motherless and had to be raised on a bottle happened to come under the special care of one of the children, who remarked that it would be a wonder if he lived. He was called Wonder.

"In naming creeks a chance circumstance would forever settle it. Father had a tussle with a wounded deer — a very large buck — one morning. The deer gave the peculiar whistle or snort so common to his kind. The little hollow was, and is until this day, called Buck Snort."

Talking about rawhide, James says: "During the Civil War and until long after Reconstruction Days, it was a saying that a Texan could take a butcher knife and rawhide and make a steamboat. He might not have been able to make a boiler, but when it came to the top part he would have been at home. One thing certain, if the thing had broken to pieces, he could have tied it up with rawhide."

Lately, self-elected authorities on cowboy life have been insisting that cowboys began wearing, and still wear, high-heeled boots for utilitarian purposes — to keep their feet from sliding through the stirrup, to enable them to "plow" the ground better when an animal roped in the pen pulls forward and the cowboy sets back with his end of the rope looped around his upper hips. This explanation has always struck me as theorizing bunk. Your bold and daring young cowboy always has been strong on style. W. S. James attributes high heels on cowboy boots to "the same motive that prompts girls to wear the opera heel."

Unlike many lovers of range life, James does not idealize the cowboy. He considers ranch people the salt of the earth and stands up for them as his own kind, but he does not picture them in moonlight or under stage light. His light is unfiltered sunlight. Going back a long generation, he says: "Let a crowd of drunken men board a train in any town in Texas, begin to whoop and yell like a troop of Comanche Indians on the warpath, and every passenger who is not posted will talk about the 'cowboys,' when perhaps not one in the roistering outfit ever saw the interior of a Texas cow camp; and yet, every such character will gladly pose as 'cowboy.' "

Everybody knows that old cowboy song, beautiful in both words and tune and rich in the metaphor of the range:

> *Last night as I lay on the prairie*
> *And looked at the stars in the sky,*
> *I wondered if ever a cowboy*
> *Would drift to that sweet by and by.*
> *They say there will be a great roundup*
> *Where cowboys like dogies shall stand*
> *To be cut by the riders of Judgment,*
> *Who are posted and know every brand.*

The last chapter in James's *Cowboy Life in Texas* is called "Lecture to Cattlemen." It is a sermon preached on the theme of this song, and it ends with a song on the same theme that James claims to have written. The religion in the sermon is so unpretentious, so genuine and sincere that a person wonders how a politician who profanes truth by using religion as a hobbyhorse ever gets by with it.

Don Quixote of the Six-Shooter

A FTER all these years the populace still regards Billy the Kid and other bad men of his kind as representative cowboys — even if a little extreme. Billy the Kid, it is true, rode well, stealing from John Chisum, who had him hired, and then from any owner whose cattle or horses were stealable. That he was a good hand, interested in his work — as all good hands at any business must be — has never been intimated. His reputation is based solely on his efficiency as killer and thief.

Sam Bass rode up the trail with a herd of cattle. At the end of the trail he helped rob a train, and the rest of his short life was spent in evading officers of the law — until they shot him. Before he went up the trail he had done odd jobs, stolen horses from the Indians, and made something of a reputation at racing "the Denton mare." He did very little cow work, and probably no real cowman would have cared for his services.

You can go up and down the list of the more noted bad men of the West — Billy the Kid, Sam Bass, John Wesley Hardin, Ben Thompson, the Daltons — and while you will find most of them associated sporadically with cowboy life, you will hardly find a dyed-in-the-wool, straight-out cowboy among them. Of course, there were plenty of tough *hombres* among both range owners and "hired men on horseback." More of them shot to hold what they had than shot to get what they held. Like other moral lines, the line between good range men who shot bad men and thieves, and bad men who rode the range was not always distinct; it often wavered. Many a cowboy was like the one in the song who says, "I know I've done wrong." But here I am talking about conduct, while Clay Allison of the Washita waits impatiently to ride and shoot.

Clay Allison is not to be classed as a gunman, either on the side of the law, like Wild Bill Hickok, or outside of the law, like John Wesley Hardin. Yet he was emphatically a man of guns. He was not a bad man in the sense that that term has come to have. Yet he seems to have killed more men than many a bad man made his reputation on. Charlie Siringo credits him with having killed eighteen; others say he killed only nine or ten. All agree that everybody he killed deserved killing. To quote from my old-time trail-driver friend, Bob Beverly of Lovington, who has supplied me a lot of data on this character, Clay Allison was "a gentleman killer." He was strictly a range man; he hated cow thieves and nobody ever accused him of being one. He was quixotic in standing up for his rights, and he was quixotically independent in interpreting what constituted his rights. The more whiskey he drank, the more rights he possessed; and sometimes when he came to town he bought a great deal of whiskey. He was generous with it, however, even insisting on his horse enjoying a fair portion.

Born in Tennessee, he was about twenty years old when the Civil War started. He was a fighting secessionist and fought through a good part of the Civil War under General Nathan Bedford Forrest. He won the reputation of being deadly accurate with the bowie knife. Once, it is told, he was captured as a spy and sentenced to be shot. But he slipped the handcuffs off over hands that were remarkably small, and lived to fight many other days.

He never was reconstructed, and in maturer years was described as looking the part of a Southern plantation gentleman. In his prime he was six feet, two inches tall, erect, weighing around 180 pounds, always neatly dressed. When he came to town he rode either a pure white or a coal black horse. After the war he went west, ranching in Colorado, New Mexico and Texas. He had made "the reputation that comes when fellers shoot" before he located on the Washita River in the Texas Panhandle, late in the seventies. He was well known in the Indian Territory and in Dodge City, where he had a notable run-in with Marshal Wyatt Earp. He died in New Mexico about 1884.

The episode in his career that has been most often related — with many variations — was his meeting with a desperado named Chunk Colbert at the Clifton House, a stage stand, in northern New Mexico. He did not know Chunk, but Chunk knew him. Chunk wanted fresh laurels to add to his reputation. Killing Clay Allison would put the biggest kind of feather in his cap. He did not conceal his ambition. Yet he was wary, and Clay was wise.

Not long after the two met, Chunk complimented Clay Allison's horse and proposed a race. The challenge was accepted, and, to Clay's chagrin, his horse was beaten. Chunk seems not to have been becomingly reticent over the victory, and Clay slapped his jaws. Night came and then bedtime, and still no gun had been drawn. When Allison went down to breakfast next morning, he found Chunk already seated at the table. With a polite salutation, he sat down directly opposite him. He had reason to think that Chunk's six-shooter was in his lap, under a napkin. A plate of scrambled eggs was set before each man. Chunk requested Allison to pass the salt, which was off to one side. When Allison reached for it, Chunk raised his six-shooter, but he fumbled the shot, and before he could shoot a second time he had a bullet between his eyes. It is related that Clay Allison finished his breakfast and walked out — to make proper funeral arrangements.

No preacher or priest was within reach, but Allison insisted on a Christian funeral. Finally he found a young man named Bill Robinson who had an Episcopalian prayer book that his mother had given him. Bill agreed to read the proper prayer over the corpse provided the nickname of "Parson" or "Preacher" was not fastened to him. He was new in the country and did not want to get tagged with any such name.

Clay Allison readily agreed to this. At the funeral he got up and said, "Friends, mourners and others, Bill Robinson here is going to give the late Chunk Colbert a decent Christian burial. This is on condition, however, that nobody will ever allude to him as Parson, Preacher, or any other such name. Now, I want you all to understand this and to realize that I am under obligation to see that his request is complied with."

Nobody ever violated the request. Edgar Beecher Bronson, in his book *The Red-Blooded,* tells another story of Clay Allison's religious proclivities. I am sure that the language ascribed by Bronson to Allison was not in character, for Allison, according to all accounts, used correct English. The story is probably more of what might have been than what was; but it is a sample of many Clay Allison stories.

One morning, as Bronson tells, Clay Allison walked into the Lone Wolf Saloon at Pecos City, liquored, laid two pistols within handy reach on the bar, and remarked to Red Dick, the bartender, that he intended to turn the saloon into a church for about two hours and that during the services he wanted no drinks sold or cards shuffled.

Then, standing at the door, one of the six-shooters in hand, Mr. Allison began to usher in the congregation. All passers were stopped. Merchants, railroad builders, gamblers, cowboys, freighters — they all knew Clay Allison. When fifty or sixty souls had assembled, he closed the door and faced about.

"Fellers," he began, "this meeting being held on the Pecos, I reckon we'll open her by singing 'Shall We Gather at the River?' Of course we are already gathered, but the song sorter fits. Now turn loose."

The result was not encouraging, for not many of the audience knew any hymn, much less this one. However, Mr. Clay Allison of the Washita was not fazed.

"The next in order," he said, "is a prayer. Everybody down!"

To quote Edgar Beecher Bronson:

Only a few knelt. Among the congregation were some who regarded the affair as sacrilegious, and others of the independent frontier type who were unaccustomed to dictation. However, a slight narrowing of the cold blue eyes and a significant sweep of the six-shooter brought every man of them to his knees, with heads bowed over faro lay-out and on monte tables.

"O Lord!" began Allison, "this yere's a mighty bad neck o' woods, an' I reckon You know it. Fellers don't think enough o' their souls to build a church, an' when a pa'son comes here they don't treat him half white. O Lord! make these fellers see that when they gits caught in the final round-up an' drove over the last divide, they don' stan' no sort o' show to git to stay on the heavenly ranch 'nless they believes an' builds a house to pray an' preach in. Right here I subscribes a hundred dollars to build a church, an' if airy one o' these yere fellers don' ante up accordin' to his means, O Lord, make it Your pers'n'l business to see that he wears the Devil's brand and earmark an' never gits another drop o' good spring water.

"Of course, I allow You knows I don' sport no wings myself, but I want to do what's right ef You'll sort o' give me a shove the proper way. An' one thing I want You to understan'; Clay Allison's got a fast horse an' is tol'able handy with his rope, and he's goin' to run these fellers into Your corral even if he has to rope an' drag 'em there. Amen. Everybody git up!"

The sermon that followed had to do with Jonah in the belly of the whale. After seeing that all hands were raised to signify belief in this Bible story, Clay Allison had Red Dick pass the hat for money to build a church. The contributions were generous and general.

In the region of Pecos, Texas, Clay Allison did another good deed. Riding into a cow camp one evening, he noticed that a young man who had a crippled arm and hand seemed very nervous. He learned that this youth had had a falling out that afternoon with another cowboy over a maverick yearling, each claiming it. They had agreed to shoot it out the next morning at a certain spot between two cow camps, the opponent's camp being over a hill. Allison told the cripple that he could never get his gun out in time and that he would take his place. So the next morning Clay Allison rode forth. He was well known to the second party of the quarrel, and when this second party galloped up, raising his gun to fire, and saw who was opposing him, he wheeled so rapidly to ride in the opposite direction that he dropped his gun. He left it behind.

Allison could be depended on to be for the underdog. A cowman himself, he took the part of farmer squatters against the strong-armed, organized cowmen.

In the old town of Cimarron, New Mexico, Allison did many of his bold deeds. Here, in the St. James Hotel billiard room, he killed Pancho Griego, who while pretending to fan himself with his hat was working to get his six-shooter out of the holster. Mace Bowman was sheriff here and wanted to take Allison into custody. This was against Allison's principles. Finally they agreed to put their six-shooters on the bar of the saloon that constituted the main part of Lambert's Hotel, each man to turn his back on the other, walk twenty-five steps, wheel, rush back to his gun and shoot. Allison specialized in odd duels. One time, as the story goes, he and his adversary agreed to dig a grave jointly, then to stand up at either end and shoot it out, the victor to cover up the other. The result of this duel was another Christian burial at which Allison was master of ceremonies. But he was crippled from a bullet that he had accidentally put into his own foot; sometimes he used his rifle for a crutch. Only on a horse was he without handicap, and it seems odd that he should have agreed with Mace Bowman to make the footrace.

He won the race, however, and his pistol was pointed straight when Bowman stuck out his chest, hit it with his fist, and said, "Shoot, you blank of a blank." Still holding his gun steady, Allison replied, "Mace, you are too brave a man to kill." The two shook hands, and the law was satisfied.

Considering his cavalier career, Clay Allison's end was pure irony. In Toyah, Texas, on a spree, he heard that two men named Joe Nash and Jake Owens were trying to get possession of his water over the New Mexico line and had made talk about him. He got a buggy and team from the livery stable and started out to find them. After driving about twenty miles, he came, at dark, to the camp made by a freighter for the Hash-knife outfit. He knew that the Hashknives were working the range and he supposed that Joe Nash and Jake Owens were probably with them. The freighter said they were; moreover, he knew where the chuck wagon was camped.

Nothing would do Clay Allison then but for the freighter to get in his buggy, drive to the Hashknife camp and warn Nash and Owens to prepare to meet their God. The freighter got back about daylight next morning, having driven all night and delivered the message. There was no road to travel, just a direction, sometimes a trail, across the prairies. The wagon was going the same way as Clay Allison for a good part of the distance.

After the four mules had been hitched to the loaded wagon, Allison proposed that he tie his buggy horses, so that they would lead, to the back of the wagon; that the freighter lie down on the load and get some sleep, and that he (Allison) get in the seat and drive. Perhaps the freighter was entirely willing; perhaps Clay Allison still had enough whiskey in him to make his arguments persuasive. Anyhow, the freighter went to sleep and Clay Allison went to driving. Before long, one of the front wheels hit a clump of salt grass, causing such a jerk and lurch that Allison was thrown off the wagon and almost under it. This scared the mules and they gave a lunge that pulled one rear wheel over Allison's head, crushing the skull and killing him instantly.

An Austin friend who dislikes having his name posted, though it is a good name, has supplied me with the following Clay Allison anecdotes.

Some fifty years ago, many stories about Clay Allison were in circulation around Pecos and other points in west Texas and New Mexico. One of these yarns related to a duel between Clay and another cowman over a water hole. In Clay Allison's day, water wells were nonexistent in vast areas of west Texas and New Mexico. Grazing land without a dependable supply of water was useless. Clay Allison and his neighboring rancher agreed on a plan to settle the controversy. In accordance with their agreement, they met at the water hole, each armed with a bowie knife, a pick and a shovel. Working together, they dug a grave. When the grave was finished they got in it, clasped left hands, and at the count of three drew their bowie knives. Clay won the battle, whereupon, according to agreement, he climbed out of the grave, filled it up, rounded it off nicely, bowed his head in a word of prayer for the deceased, then mounted his horse and went on his way. That was Clay Allison's story, according to the old-timers around Pecos, and as he was the only witness and was not present to question the testifiers, there was no one to dispute the story. Nor is there anyone to dispute my friend's telling, which looks like a variant of the Mace Bowman story.

Another legend purports to relate the facts about the effort of a sheriff at Las Vegas, New Mexico, to arrest Clay on a warrant charging some infraction of the law. According to the story, the sheriff, with the warrant in his pocket, got in his buggy and drove out from Las Vegas to a place where Clay Allison was camped. Clay evidently saw him coming, for he rode toward him on his horse. The sheriff sat in his buggy and read the warrant to Clay, who listened attentively. When the sheriff told him he was under arrest, Clay said, "Okay," and started riding along at a slow pace, the sheriff following in his buggy. A mile or two before they reached Las Vegas, a skunk crossed the road in front of Clay. He pulled his gun and killed it, got off his horse, picked up the dead skunk, walked to the buggy and disarmed the sheriff.

He cut off a piece of saddle string and tied one end of it around the animal's neck and the other to its feet, and hung it around the sheriff's neck. Under Clay's orders, the sheriff drove around the square with Clay following behind, shouting, "Look, fellows, the sheriff's got me under arrest." After circling the square, Clay waved to the spectators, put the steel to his horse, and loped out of town.

He was one range man exceedingly deft with a six-shooter who was not a bad man. Other men much less interesting have had whole books written about them. He seems more of a storyteller's character than a biographer's. The most delicate points of the code of the West could be drawn from his career.

Men of Babícora

NEWSPAPERS and weeklies have been carrying releases on the sale of the William Randolph Hearst ranch, La Babícora, in Chihuahua to the Mexican government. I visited it a little over eighteen years ago. I imagine it has not changed much since then. Change will come when the Mexican government sells it off in small tracts to farmers. When I visited the ranch the *agraristas* had seized about 100,000 acres and had been virtually stopped. Over a million acres were left, of which the most valuable formed a roughly circular basin of about 400,000 acres. There never was better grassland than this mile-or-more-high plateau-basin.

My friend Kelly Simmons, *administrador* (general manager) of Babícora, had invited me to come and stay as long as I would. He had been manager of a sugar plantation and mill in the state of Sinaloa and knew Mexico and Mexican ways. He was an urbane and gracious gentleman with a soft voice and gentle manners. I wanted to be with him, be on the big hacienda, and learn.

My original plan was to go to El Paso, cross the river, and take the Mexican Northwestern train, which was mixed and ran only in daylight, to Madera, where a ranch car would meet me. Then, early in January of the year 1935, I received a telegram from Simmons to meet him in El Paso.

It is about 300 miles, south and west, from El Paso to Babícora headquarters. Simmons was driving his car through but turned me over to a Yaqui Indian named Lupe Quijada, who was manager of the Nahuerichic subdivision of the ranch and who had come up to El Paso to spend the Christmas–New Year holidays. I have made pack trips across the Sierra Madre of Chihuahua, Sonora, and Durango and been on some of the big haciendas of northwestern Mexico, but this Lupe Quijada, who introduced me to La Babícora, somehow expressed in himself the vastness and silences, the life unseen as well as seen, of the mountains, canyons, and plateaus to which he was born as no other man I have met. Of himself he told me very little, but he was so positive in nature that one absorbed from him. Kelly Simmons and others told me a good deal.

He said he would be awaiting me at the Rio Bravo Hotel in Juarez at ten-thirty on the morning of January 7. I judged that he meant *tiempo Americano* and not *tiempo Mexicano,* "American time" meaning promptness. I had never experienced delays of any consequence in getting a tourist permit into Mexico or getting through any border customs office, but I was plenty early in taking a cab at the Paso del Norte Hotel in El Paso. I wore boots and other ranch gear and had a bedroll, a typewriter, and a small grip.

While the taxicab ticked away in front of the immigration offices on the Mexican side of the Rio Grande, I presented myself for a permit. The tight-mouthed clerk gave me a searching look and asked my name. I told him. He asked me if I had any means of identifying myself. I pulled out the telegram from Kelly Simmons. My occupation? Professor at the University of Texas and writer, I responded.

"What is your business at La Babícora?" he asked.

"I am going on a vacation, to learn the country, to make a pack trip from there across the Sierras and perhaps to write something," I responded.

"Yes," he rejoined, "and to buy cattle."

"No," I explained, "I am not a cattle buyer, even if I am ranchero by rearing and am dressed ranchero style."

Abruptly, the clerk turned from me to scribble on various cards and papers that lay on his desk. I stood humbly waiting. A few minutes later he beckoned me to come into the hall. "You are a cow buyer," he said, "and I am going to make you admit it."

"No, I am not a cow buyer, but if it will help matters for me to say that I am, then have it that way."

"I will see the chief." He left me standing in the hall and entered the room of the chief inspector of immigration. Soon he reappeared. "We cannot issue you a tourist permit," he announced.

Out in the taxi I had two books of my own authorship that I was carrying down to present to my host. I went and fetched them. "You have my name and occupation," I said. "Look at these books I have written."

"Then," he remarked with the coolness of infallibility, "you are going to La Babícora to sell books."

I could hardly resist shouting in glee. "Figure to yourself," I said, "how would it pay me to journey all the way to La Babícora to sell two books at a dollar each. I should like to speak to the chief myself."

"It is impossible. He is occupied."

That seemed to settle the matter. I stood to heel for two or maybe three minutes longer. Then I made for the office of the American consul. He knew me. I explained the situation. He talked to the chief over the telephone, made emphatic assurances of my character and occupation. Then, having given his word that I would buy no cattle, he received the promise of a tourist permit for me. I returned and got it.

The Mexican officials were not without reason. In order to do business in Mexico a foreigner must post a bond and get a kind of commercial passport that costs considerably more than a tourist permit. Various cow buyers from New Mexico and Texas had been getting tourist permits and going down into Chihuahua to trade. Another of these posing as a writer was not going to put anything over on them.

Lupe Quijada was awaiting me. At that time he was about fifty years old, as straight as an arrow and lithe as a panther, weighing not more than 125 pounds. I do not know how as a full-blooded Yaqui he had gone to Santa Clara College in California. He told me, in answer to a question, that he had studied French and Greek. His English was correct, though strongly accented. His dark eyes, I thought, might bore into the heart of a mesquite post. As I saw him later on his own range, I noticed how he seemed to blend with the ground like a deer or a wild turkey. He appeared and disappeared without seeming to come or go. I write of him as of the past, for I have not seen or heard of him now for eighteen years.

He was the most silent of all animated men I have met. While I was at La Babícora, a Mormon from Casas Grandes brought his wife and stayed there with her for two days. During all that time she spoke not a single word that I heard. At the table, if asked if she would have some of this or that, she merely reached in response. The silence of Guadalupe Quijada was a very different silence from that of the Mormon woman. Its source was not timidity or lack of interest or vitality. It was the silence of strength in repose, of reserve power, of life itself. Also, it seemed to me, the silence of contempt. Like Jesse James in the old song, Quijada "came of a solitary race." All he wanted was to be left alone.

Kelly Simmons told me that more than once he had driven to Lupe Quijada's division quarters with a determination to outsilence him. They might sit for two hours in front of the burning fireplace or on the gallery gazing away at mountains. Finally, although he must have known that not another soul was within ten kilometers, Quijada would begin looking, this way and that way, all around. Then in a whisper he would begin to say something, a whisper that was not exactly a whisper either — a tone as low as that of the doe warning her fawn not to be curious. Once started in this talk of security and confidence, Quijada might talk for a long hour to the administrador.

As a youth, Quijada used to make trips across the Sierra Madre from ranches in Sonora to Chihuahua, sometimes driving horses or cattle, sometimes trailing thieves, often alone with only a mozo. I can imagine his being out with a mozo for a century and never saying a word to him beyond an order. One day, after a silence of about two hours, having looked all around to see that no other person was within ten miles, he gave Kelly Simmons this account in his laconic English.

"Many times on a trip across the Sierra Madre I sat alone all night by the fire drinking coffee, looking. I

saw things sometimes in the darkness that I did not know
if they were real or not. The fire it is a thinker, a
silencer. It makes shadows; it reveals strange things.

"One night I was sitting late, late by the fire, drinking
a little coffee now and then, my mozo asleep on the other
side. I did not see anything, but I felt something. I cannot tell why. I move to one side very easy. I awake the
mozo without speaking. I order him to follow me, very
quietly. We go out, then we make circle. I find where
two Apaches have been hiding and watching me.

"Those Apaches they follow me one, two, three days.
I cannot tell why. Once only I see them — just like that,"
and Quijada pointed a finger into first one and then the
other of his eyes. "From then on, after I make the fire
at night, I move to one side."

John Williams, range boss at the Babícora, with Quijada and a *vaquero,* was trailing four horse thieves. Close
to sundown they reached a mountain overlooking a well-
grassed and well-watered canyon in which they felt sure
the thieves were camped. Williams decided to camp up
in the mountain and go down in the early morning for
a surprise attack.

They camped. Very early they trailed out, Williams
in front, the Mexican next, Quijada behind. After they
had gone a distance and the light of dawn was showing,
Williams looked back. "Where is Quijada?" he asked.
The Mexican looked back. He did not know. Quijada
had said nothing. He had just disappeared. The two
hesitated to go on without him. While they were still
waiting for Quijada to come up, he appeared in front
of them driving the four thieves, their hands up, his
gun on them. He had somehow caught a swift glimpse
of them doubling back on their trail, had slipped about

so as to get the drop on them, and now had them. It was like him to say nothing, to make no explanation, either before or after his action.

Sometimes more than a year would pass without Quijada's putting foot inside the Babícora headquarters. His business was to tend to the Nahuerichic division. If the ranch management had business with him, very well; he had none with the management. Before becoming division superintendent, he had been *caporal* (boss) for the main corrida of vaqueros. He would stay with them for two or three years before coming in to draw his pay. This he invested. When I met him he owned a ranch of his own and a home, where his family lived, in El Paso. He erected to his father, buried in the cemetery at Chihuahua City, an impressive monument. I do not know when his people pulled away from the Yaqui tribe.

His pride was not Mexican. It was a little that of the Spaniard; it was far more that of the Indian. Punctiliously courteous, he deferred to no human being. As we rode south from El Paso into the Chihuahua desert, we made little talk. I asked some questions — none personal. They were answered quietly and finally, no door being left open into which to enter for an exchange of ideas or experiences.

The highway from El Paso to Chihuahua City is paved now. It was then little more than a wagon road. Fifty miles out, a terrific norther hit us with a blasting sandstorm. The dust was so thick that at times we could not see across the road. Once we stopped and stood still for a quarter of an hour. About three o'clock we reached Villa Ahumada, some 80 miles from Juarez and the first settlement of more than railroad section hands south of the Rio Grande.

Here we got whiskey and lunch. The bottle I presented to Quijada seemed to take a kink out of his back. The lunch cost 60 centavos each — about 17 cents. It consisted of a meat soup, a meat stew — tough bull meat — a *sopa* of crackers, frijoles, and coffee.

We drove on. The wind and sand kept blowing. A gringo in a car off to one side of the road jumped out waving and yelling frantically. He ran to us. Out of breath, he asked, "Do you speak American?"

"Certainly," Quijada responded.

The gringo was driving on a rim, and his radiator had run out of water. He had with him wife, mother-in-law, and three children. He had run into a Mexican's car, a head-on collision, just down the road. He asked how far it was to Villa Ahumada. Quijada told him two or three miles. I knew it to be five miles if a rod. I said nothing. As we drove on, Quijada said, "I do not wish to be *testigo* — witness — in this car wreck matter."

We found the Mexican's car standing in the road a short distance away. He, his womenfolk and children all stood out in the wind, their backs to the blasting sands. They were afraid to get in the car for fear another traveler would run into them. We did not stop.

We passed some shipping pens into which men were crowding a herd of cows. At dark we reached Gellego, where the shipping pens were full of calves to be shipped to the United States. We ate supper in a one-room shack. It consisted of meat soup, tortillas and lightbread, chile con carne, and frijoles either with or without chile, and coffee. The price was 70 centavos.

At two o'clock in the morning, after having been on the road for fourteen and a half hours, traversing three hundred miles, we reached the Hacienda Babícora. Quijada said that if he could get gasoline he would go on to his ranch, thirty miles away. I think he was tired, though he would not admit to being so. Manager Simmons came out and asked Quijada to stay all night so that they might talk business a little in the morning. He stayed. He was up before daylight drinking coffee — his entire breakfast.

The hacienda was operated in four divisions. La Babícora, general headquarters, was at the same time a division. It was under the management of John Williams ("Don Juan Chaves"), a "Jack Mormon," who also had charge of cow work over the entire range. He had come to the Sierra Madre when he was a child and had seen Apaches kill the wife and son of a neighbor. He had ridden with the peon vaqueros of Governor Terrazas — who once owned and controlled many millions of Chihuahua acres — when all they had to eat was dried beef and fresh beef. He had been at Babícora thirty years and could have told a book on it. He talked in a slow, gentle tone, often smiling and occasionally winking an eye at some invisible listener beside him.

I have already sketched Lupe Quijada, the lone-wolf superintendent of the Nahuerichic division. Las Varas, on the Northwestern Railroad, was under a man named McKay. He was married to a half-breed Mexican woman and his children spoke no English. He was responsible for road work, farming, and the upkeep of fences over the entire ranch.

The fourth division, Santa Ana, is twenty-five miles or so southeast of headquarters, across the continental divide from the other three divisions. It is something separate. For me it had an atmosphere of greater an-

tiquity and of more remoteness from change. Gus Mc-
Ginnis, the superintendent, came to Mexico about 1901
as a cowboy for the T O outfit, with which he was also
windmiller and carpenter. He had studied law a little
in the States. His special function now was to deal with
Mexican lawyers, politicians, and agrarians. He had
married a Mexican woman and raised children by her.
I noticed that he always spoke to his son Bob in Spanish,
although Bob had studied aviation in the States, was a
radio fiend, and spoke fluent English. While thoroughly
Mexicanized in many ways, Gus McGinnis had retained
his American perspective and continued to read history.

One day while I was at Santa Ana, he received a wire
to go to Juarez and give the hacienda bookkeeper there
power of attorney for a trip to Mexico City to fight im-
position of 30,000 pesos for back income taxes. He and
I had just met the weekly mail from Temosachic (on the
railroad) to Namiquipa. This mail was carried on a
burro driven by an old man afoot.

Cárdenas was president of Mexico at this time, and
the parceling out of great haciendas to the agrarians was
in full blast. Cárdenas had recently said in a speech that
the only great estate remaining for parceling out in Chihuahua was La Babícora. Kelly Simmons and Gus Mc-
Ginnis were perpetually busy with agrarian claimants
and political manipulators. Only the power of the
Hearst press in the United States saved Babícora to
private ownership.

The Babícora laborers were not themselves turning
agrarian. They had been far better treated than the
peonized laborers on nearly all of the Mexican-owned
haciendas. They were called *mascarillas* — white-faces,
mascaria being the Mexican name for white-faced cattle

— the Babícora breed. They were also taunted as *agringados* — gringo-lovers.

In 1935 about 300 men were on the Babícora payroll. I don't know what wages the mechanics and artisans received. There were many of them: drivers and maintainers of tractors and automobiles, blacksmiths, carpenters, leather workers, who made all saddles and harness used on the ranch, and other specialists.

The vaqueros and field hands drew 45 pesos (about 13 American dollars, according to the then current rate of exchange) a month, plus found. This consisted of coffee, sugar, beef, beans, chili, bread of both wheat and corn, and vermicelli (for sopa). Mexican ranches in the country were paying less and not furnishing coffee, sugar or beef. Married vaqueros on the Babícora were allowed plots of land to plant in corn, wheat, and beans. The land was broken for them by ranch machinery and they were furnished seed, teams, and implements; in return they gave half the crop to the ranch. The management did not want to farm but had to.

In gathering cattle, the cow outfits from two or three divisions generally joined forces, each maintaining its wagon. Cattle ranging in the mountains were driven to and worked on the open flat country, where camp was kept.

Along about four o'clock in the afternoon, each of twenty or thirty vaqueros would get a little dried meat or fresh beef, a dozen tortillas, and some coffee and sugar. A tin cup was tied to every saddle. Then all would ride ten or twelve miles back into the mountains, there separating by twos and threes. Each pair or trio would stake horses, always with hair ropes. Then they would build up a fire, cook meat, boil coffee, warm over the tortillas, and pass the night. Just before daylight they would string out for the flats, pushing cattle ahead, combing a big country. By eight or nine o'clock they would have the roundup together, change horses, eat, and go to working on the herd.

It is always cold on the heights. The vaqueros took no blankets, had no slickers — only a serape apiece. It might be raining. If so, they would keep fires going all night and get little sleep.

The caporal (wagon boss) that I came closest to was Res Talivera, of the Santa Ana division, another man of silence and iron. He was hard and cruel but never harsh to a horse. He was a great horse trainer, but relied on mules for cow work in rough mountain country. He worked his men sixteen hours a day and on Sundays. He seldom spoke to one except to give an order. While they garrulously ate around the wagon, he ate to one side in silence. He slept to one side. He was always looking. He could barely read and write, but knew what to do, never asking for orders but taking them when given.

"I have been riding with Res Talivera in the mountains," Kelly Simmons told me, "and noted a buck. 'That is the biggest buck we have seen in two or three days,' I might say. 'I saw three back yonder that were bigger,' Talivera would reply. 'Why didn't you say something about it?' A shrug of the shoulders would be the only answer. There are things inside him. He will die with them there."

Pedro Lopez was not in the least like the silent men of Babícora whom I have sketched. He was as big as a skinned mule, big-mouthed, swart and good-natured, without any suggestion of spiritual or intellectual quality in his features. Pedro Lopez looked cunning and he was cunning, not in a slippery way but in a bold, brazen, knock-down way.

For a good many years he had been the chief law enforcer of La Babícora. He held a kind of high sheriff's commission from the governor of Chihuahua and had four subsheriffs under him. He was also judge and jury. By tradition in Mexico, these functions are practically, though not so stipulated by law, combined in the military, *rurales* (rangers), and such special "peace officers" as Pedro Lopez. He had probably killed, "they said," seventy-five men — in the line of duty. If a man was known to be guilty, why waste time on judges and juries and fool with lawyers and the formalities of law? Pedro did not shoot all the criminals he apprehended. Sometimes, if he felt like it, he beat one into a jelly with an old sword he carried.

Not long before I visited La Babícora, the Hearst representative from California, who was over all Hearst ranch properties in that state and in Mexico, arrived at Babícora by plane. It happened that manager Kelly Simmons and his wife were both away. The California representative was accompanied by his wife, and they occupied the rooms usually occupied by Mr. and Mrs. Simmons. Early in the morning after their arrival they stepped out of their bedroom onto a wide veranda to walk to breakfast. They did not notice the bodies of two dead men in front of their door until they had stepped on them. The lady screamed and fainted. The two receded into their room and barricaded the door with furniture. As soon as possible they got to their plane and flew back to El Paso.

Those dead Mexicans were the handiwork of Pedro

Lopez. After being on their trail for months, one night he apprehended them at a gate leading out of the ranch domain, and with the assistance of two subsheriffs, filled them full of lead. He thought that the *patrón* would appreciate looking at the evidence. He drove on into the Babícora in the night and deposited the evidence of his efficiency on the floor in front of the door that his boss would walk out of the next morning. He did not know that the patrón was away.

One time while he and another officer of his kind were at a dance in Guerrero, this fellow officer advised him that a man named Alfred Pena was wanted for murder in the mining camp of Namiquipa across the mountains. "And yonder Alfred Pena is," the fellow officer pointed. "He confesses to the name."

Warrants for arrest are not necessary in Mexico. Pedro and his *compadre* seized the alleged Alfred Pena. The man declared that he had not only never killed a man but had never been in Namiquipa. That made no difference. All criminals are liars. Pedro and his fellow took him to the *presidente* of Namiquipa, explaining they were doing him a favor. "It's true," the presidente said, "that one Alfred Pena killed a man in this municipality and is wanted for murder. But this is not the right Alfred Pena. We know nothing about him."

Reluctantly, the prisoner was released. He became abusive of his captors. They killed him and put his body in a well. Complaints against Pedro Lopez were lodged with the governor by the presidente. Pedro Lopez went to the governor. He explained how the mistake came up; he added that if this Alfred Pena did not deserve killing for a murder in Namiquipa, he deserved it for something else and on general principles. In view of

Pedro's remarkable record for efficiency, the governor excused him. A little later the presidente at Namiquipa was going about telling how a man from Guerrero by the name of Alfred Pena had come to Namiquipa one night and stumbled into a well and killed himself. If the military or other police officers are overzealous and take the lives of the innocent along with the guilty, it is to be remembered that "God will sort the souls."

Away to the northwest of Babícora, Mormons established colonies late in the last century. A Mormon rancher named Dave Brown, a giant six feet six, came to Kelly Simmons one time and told him that thieves were stealing his cattle faster than he could raise them. He wanted to borrow Pedro Lopez.

"I'll be glad for you to have Pedro," Simmons said, "but we don't have any power to transfer him. Go to the governor and get his permission and then Pedro will help you out."

Dave Brown went to the governor. Certainly the cow thieving should be stopped. Pedro Lopez was ordered to the assistance of the Mormon. Dave Brown thought that this would be a good time to visit his daughter in El Paso. "I am going away," he said to Pedro. "I may be gone for considerable time. You know what you have to do. Be no respecter of persons. Stop the thieves."

Brown left. He was gone two months. One day he came tearing into the Babícora. "My God," he said, "get Pedro Lopez back here where he belongs."

"What's the matter? Hasn't he caught the thieves yet?" Simmons asked.

"Caught them? He is ruining me. He has killed two of my sons-in-law."

"Were they guilty?"

"I guess they were; in fact, I am sure they were. But, man, their families are being left on my hands. If Pedro keeps on, I'll have all the people kin to me in Chihuahua living off my table. Call him home."

Pedro had been "no respecter of persons."

Of all I saw and heard at La Babícora, the sandhill cranes — *grullas* — give me most happiness in recollection. They come in from the north toward late September and start back in March. While I was there in January, men and boys were constantly scaring them out of fields of ungathered corn. I estimated just one flock in one field to number 2,000. About dusk tens of thousands gathered at the shallow *lagunas* out in the great basin-prairie to roost. One day while riding across the prairie in a car, I saw them lined alongside the road, but somewhat off, for a mile. Sandhill cranes stalk about majestical and strange; they fly grand and beautiful. I shall never forget clouds of them flying west against a smoldering sunset and fluting out their long, long cries.

An Old Trail Driver Tells His Story

THE year that Texas entered the Union as a state, W. W. Burton was two years old and his family had been in Texas thirteen years. They had planted their first corn crop by punching holes in the ground with a stick and dropping in grains of corn. Like many other thrifty families, they accumulated a stock of cattle. When Mr. Burton was eighty-three years old — that was in 1927 — I got him to tell his early range experiences.

He was living in Austin then and I came to know him through his son, Wes, who was an oldish man himself and was one of the hardest hunters after lost mines and one of the best storytellers about lost mines I ever listened to. I used to go over to the Burton house across the Colorado River in Austin about dark and not leave until after midnight. Most of the time I was just listening. There was a blind daughter in the family, named Pinkey, and she would play a pump organ and sing old ballads, the rest joining in. Mrs. Burton had seen a ghost out in their yard several times and she liked to point out a dark spot on the floor in the kitchen made by blood from the murdered man — fifty years past. The whole Burton family was made out of bedrock kindness and goodness and hospitality. They had very little in the way of property, but they were contented and envied no one. They were very cheerful people, often merry.

Here I am putting down W. W. Burton's account of the old cattle days pretty much as he told it and without quotation marks.

In 1852, my father bought a ranch out from the Brazos River above the present city of Waco, and I helped drive out six hundred head of cattle to the new range. I was only eight years old then; I don't know how long I had been riding. By the time I was twelve years old I considered myself a good rider and roper.

Sam Burton, my father, believed in letting his sons have a little sense knocked into them. A horse might be pitching with Otho, my kid brother. Mother would be screaming that he was being killed, and Pa would just read on as he sat there on the gallery, never looking up. He'd simply remark, "If Otho gets throwed, it won't do him no harm. He needs a little experience anyhow."

The settlers who did not build their houses at springs or on streams dug wells by hand. But in those days we had no windmills, and we drew water only for home use and for saddle horses and milch cows. Range stock watered at lakes and streams. Sometimes we made a little tank on a draw. We had no scrapers to carry the dirt, so we used cowhides. A man or two spaded dirt onto a big dry hide; another man on horseback had his rope tied to the tail and when the hide was loaded he dragged it over to where the dam was to be made. It was easy to dump the dirt by pulling the hide back and over instead of straight forward. After the toughest ox hide had been dragged around in this manner for a while, it became as pliable as buckskin. Mother took two or three such soft hides from us boys and used them to place under mattresses. They were as warm as buffalo robes.

We had no horseshoes to speak of. If a horse went lame from being tenderfooted, we might turn him loose and catch another. But often we were where we couldn't let the horse go without risk of never finding him again. Then the remedy was to take a hot iron and sear the tender part of the foot. It never seemed to hurt much. Many a time I've set a horse's foot down on a red-hot skillet lid, and he'd hold it there till I took him away. After that he'd mend up, and in two or three days I'd be riding him again.

Taking cattle through a rough country would make some of them tenderfooted, and on a drive to Missouri in 1859, we threw down some big steers and burned their feet and they got all right. Of course if you burned an animal's heel too high up it would get lamer, and I've heard of cattle rustlers burning a cow's feet to keep her from following a calf they were driving off and then burning the calf's feet after they reached a holding place in order to keep it from going back.

In those days the ranches in various counties were numbered. Our ranch was Number Seven, McLennan County. I knew most of the ranchers for a hundred miles in each direction from us, though the country to the north was sparsely settled. There was no cattle stealing to speak of until the Civil War. When a cowman branded his calves, he branded any other calf in the pen with the brand worn by its mother. Nearly all the branding was done by neighbors working together.

About the only cattle we sold were grown steers. When a rancher gathered his steers to sell, he caught everything else in the same class running on his range and sold them too, keeping a book account of the various brands. Once a year there would be a meeting of stockmen to settle accounts. Stockmen who did not attend would usually have a neighbor to represent them at the meeting. In time the custom grew up of depositing with the county treasurer money from the sale of stray cattle. A cowman would send his representative once a year to various county seats to collect the money that had been turned in on his brand or brands.

When beef buyers came to receive cattle, they brought along gold, sometimes in a money belt, sometimes in saddlebags, sometimes in a sack or a *morral*. While the cattle were being delivered, this money hung unprotected in camp or in some rancher's home. After the cattle were received, the gold pieces were counted out to the owner, maybe on a blanket, maybe right on the ground.

In 1859, I made my first drive up the trail, though I had been to Louisiana the year before. The herd consisted of five hundred mature steers put up by seven neighboring ranchmen, one of whom was my father. In those days there were no big outfits in our part of the country. Generally a buyer from Missouri or Louisiana came to the settlement and contracted for the beeves. In 1858 a buyer named Saunders had come in and paid $25 around for five-year-old steers, $20 for four-year-old steers and $15 for threes. However, a steer under four years old was seldom sold. This man Saunders promised to come back the next spring, but he did not show up. No other buyer came, and along in June the ranchers decided to put Mot Donahue in charge and send their beeves to Springfield, Missouri. We took a weekly newspaper published in Missouri that kept us more or less posted on prices.

Mot Donahue was the only grown man in the outfit, the other five of us being youngsters. We had four horses apiece, and the extra horses were driven right along with the cattle and herded with them. The big herds with their horse wranglers, or remuda men, were a later development.

Our cook was a Negro called Uncle Charlie, but as he belonged to Donahue he was sometimes spoken of as Charlie Donahue. He drove a wagon drawn by one pair of oxen. Soon after the Donahues came to McLennan County in 1852, Charlie had an experience he never forgot. It made him a kind of hero among the other Negroes, and I have heard him relate it a hundred times.

Mot Donahue didn't know much about Indians at the time he settled in the county, and one morning when his oxen came up missing he began to look for them. After he and his boys had ridden high and low for a day or two, my father said to him, "If you'll give those lazy Waco Indians a red handkerchief or something like that, they'll bring your oxen in. They've simply got the oxen hid out somewhere." Well, Donahue promised the Indians something if they would bring in the oxen, and, sure enough, in a little while they came bringing them in.

When they left, Donahue told them that if they saw a black boy on a black mare to tell him to come on in, as the oxen had been found. The black boy on the black mare was Charlie, and of course the Indians found him. But when he saw them coming toward him, Charlie was suspicious and took to the tall timbers. The Indians followed him with wild whoops and in no time ran him down and roped him. Then they soberly delivered their message and went on. They would have delivered that message if they had had to run the Negro into Donahue's house itself to catch him.

But to get back to the trail herd. We crossed the Trinity River at Dallas, then just a wide place in the road. We crossed Red River at Rabbit Ford, as it was then called, though later it came to be known as Colbert's Ferry. An Indian had a little ferryboat, and crossed our wagon for a dollar. The boat was not big enough to hold both the oxen and the wagon, and so the oxen had to swim with the rest of us. We were now in the Indian Nation, but everything was quiet and we had no trouble. I do not remember having seen any other cattle than ours on the trail, but the route we traveled was well marked. It was called the Old Beef Trail.

We crossed Blue River at Nail's Mill, called after a Cherokee named Nail. Our next crossing was on Boggy River. Then after crossing the Canadian and the Arkansas we came to old Fort Gibson on the Neosho, where there was a store that handled cowboy supplies. We passed Honey Springs, where there were a post office and another store. Our trail led on through Granny Gap, just a narrow pass in the Granny Mountains, and on to Springfield, a mere village then.

I don't remember what the cattle brought — probably around $50 a head. We boys had other fish to fry when we got to a town like Springfield, and left the selling to Mot Donahue. Each of us wore two six-shooters — I've got one of mine yet. We left Waco along in June and were back early in September. We drove slow going up, giving the steers plenty of time to fatten on the way. It took about two and a half months to make the trip up and about two weeks to come back. After we crossed Red River on the way home, some of us left Charlie and the chuck wagon and made good time to the Brazos.

It amuses me to see picture shows and to read articles claiming that trail driving began only after the Civil War. Our herd was by no means the first to leave central Texas for Missouri, and herds from the southern part of the state drove through our range. When we went to McLennan County in 1852, cattle were being driven north and east. I could name a dozen stockmen of our neighborhood who were driving cattle, sometimes to Shreveport, Louisiana, sometimes to Missouri. Their herds numbered from a hundred to five hundred big steers. They always took an ox wagon along, never pack outfits.

More cattle were being driven into Shreveport in the fifties than to Missouri. I went in 1858, and in 1860 went twice. Mot Donahue was in charge of the drives to Shreveport, just as he was on the drive to Missouri. It generally took us about a month to drive. The usual time for leaving McLennan County was late in August or early in September after the calf crop was branded and the steers had already fattened, but we never crowded them. A plain wagon road could be followed all the way. We crossed the Trinity River at Wildcat Crossing, about twenty miles below Corsicana; we crossed the Neches just below old Fort Nacogdoches; then we passed through Marshall and on into Shreveport.

When the cattle reached Shreveport, they were loaded on barges and taken down Red River to New Orleans and sold. The barges held forty or fifty steers each and were towed. Mot Donahue always went with our cattle on the boats, and after the cattle were loaded we boys came back home. In 1860, however, Mr. Mot left me and Archie Donahue to herd about twenty-five steers in the crabgrass around Shreveport. The steers were not fat, and Donahue instructed us to graze them until they got in better condition. He promised to be back "before long."

Well, time went on and Donahue did not show up or send any word. The steers were getting fat, and every day or two one of us would ride into Shreveport and ask Haswell, who was the chief livestock commission man, if he had heard anything. One day a couple of New Orleans buyers came out in a livery rig to look at our beeves. When we told them that we would not sell them for less than $50 around they went up in the air. "Hell, they're not worth that much in New Orleans," they said. "All right," we replied, "if you don't want 'em at $50, don't take 'em."

They went back to town, chewed the rag with Haswell, reported us as being the toughest nuts west of the Mississippi, and then came back. They offered us $50 if we would put the steers on board a barge. Our terms were $50 delivered in the pens, and after the buyers had made another bluff they traded.

About the time we delivered the cattle, Haswell got a letter from Donahue. He had found the market at New Orleans on a boom, and had taken a boat to Galveston, gone from there by stage to Waco, and now was making up a second herd to drive to Shreveport. He instructed us to sell the beeves and come home. As we had already sold them, we did not have anything to do but ride back west.

Had we known we were going to strike Donahue and

his new herd, I think we would have circled around him, for we were tired of the Louisiana climate; but, as luck would have it, we met him in the Trinity bottoms. He was having an awful time, driving short of hands, while the heel-flies chased his cattle. We had to turn around and make another trip to Shreveport.

Of course, there were no banks in those days in our part of the country, and the money we carried home was either gold or bills on a bank in New Orleans, which were as good as gold. I knew one man who bought in Shreveport a bushel of Mexican two-bit pieces at a dime each, brought them back to the Brazos, and there had no trouble in passing them at face value — two bits, or a quarter.

In the fifties a saddle pony was worth $7 or $8. Many of ours were from Mexico and had Mexican brands on them. When we got through working cattle in the fall we turned most of our horses loose on the range with the expectation of their being stolen by Indians before spring. Every spring a Mexican named Juan Sanchez brought horses up from the Rio Grande and sold them to the ranchers. The Indians who stole our horses would sometimes take them to Mexico and trade them off. In this way we had a chance of buying back our own stock.

We did not have the well-organized roundups of later days. Our work was called a cow hunt, and a cow hunt was what it was. The cowmen set a date for beginning work, met at some designated place, with not more than two or three horses each, and began hunting the cattle.

Every man was his own cook, though squads might combine. In a gathering of twenty men there might be two or three pack animals. We took enough bread with us to last a week. Sometimes a ranch woman would spend a half-day cooking bread for a crowd of cow hunters that came near her home. She might be offered pay, but the chances were she would not take it. About all the cooking any of us did was to boil coffee and roast meat over the coals. Any fat animal conveniently at hand was legitimate beef, no matter to whom it belonged.

In 1861 the Burton family branded 1,100 calves. When the war was over and brother Otho and I got home we found only two hundred calves to brand. A great deal of the stock along the Brazos had been driven west by renegades, some of whom became cattle kings. But after the war cattle were worth next to nothing anyhow. Choice steers sold at $8 and $10 a head, and stock cattle could be purchased for a dollar or two.

It was about 1867 that our neighborhood had quite a bit of excitement over a slick rascal from the North, who came in, put up at the old Peter McLennan Hotel in Waco, and bought a string of cattle from surrounding ranchers. He had his outfit with him and was away and gone with the cattle before somebody discovered that the greenback money which had been paid out for the cattle — as well as the hotel bill — was all counterfeit. A posse was made up to follow him. I remember that I was in a cow camp at the time word of the cheating reached us. I and some other men left right away to join in the hunt.

Some of the posse caught the cattle at Red River. I don't know whether the counterfeit money man went up the river or down it, but I have always understood he did not go across it. There was a saying in those days that the law of Texas was at the end of a rope. The legitimate owners of the cattle simply put one of their number in charge and sent the herd on to Kansas.

In 1868 Jim Taylor and I started for Kansas with a herd of nine hundred mixed cattle. We crossed Red River at Colbert's Ferry, where we had crossed in 1859 going to Missouri. But when we got up into the Indian Territory we met men who told us that the Indians were so bad we could not get through to Kansas. They said that Kansas was full of cattle without buyers. It was against the law for us to drive into Missouri, as Texas cattle were giving the native cattle fever. Nothing was then known about ticks being the carriers of the fever. Texas cattle simply were not wanted. All that was left for us to do was to go into Arkansas.

We went into Benton County, which corners in the northwestern part of the state against Missouri on the north and the old Indian Nation on the west. There we managed to get rid of most of the cattle somehow. We just had to peddle them out, trading off some for wagons and horses, smuggling a few heifers across the line into Missouri, and worrying along as best we could. It was December before we got home.

Smuggling cattle into Missouri was ticklish business, for the country was full of men who hated Texas cows and Texas cowmen like the devil hates holy water. We never tried to take more than fifteen or twenty head at a time and those in the night, maybe for fifteen miles. One morning a good while before daybreak I and another cowhand were riding back to Benton County after having delivered a little bunch of cattle when we heard men shooing cattle along. They were not yelling or popping whips, I want to say, but whispering to those dogies. I knew that Pete Ross, brother to Sul Ross, later governor of Texas, was holding a herd a little way below mine, and I somehow recognized his shooing.

"Here there," I yelled out in the best disguised voice I could muster, "hold up and explain where you're taking these Texas cattle. We've been looking for you."

Well, you ought to have heard that man explain. Why, his cattle had just broke a barn fence down in the night and were running away when he caught up with them and now he was taking them back home. I carried the joke on as long as I wanted to and then I told him who I was. He asked me never to tell the joke on him, but after we got back to Waco I told it every time we got in a crowd.

Our most memorable experience on the trip was swimming Red River. When we reached it we found Duckworth and Scaling of Hill County, with a herd of two thousand mixed cattle. They had been trying for three days to get their cattle across and were still trying. A scalawag living in the neighborhood claimed that he was an expert at crossing cattle, and they were hiring him by the day to point the cattle across. His practice was to ride in a little upstream and then, about the time the lead cattle were well out in the water, to drift down and head them back. He claimed that he could not hold his horse or something, but as an expert riverman he was getting a fancy price every day and he was making the job last.

Duckworth had heard that we were coming and had sent back word for us to hold our cattle out from the river, which we did. I went on down, and the first thing I said was, "You call yourself a cowman, do you?"

"Now, don't try to guy me," said Duckworth. "I'm a cowman and you know it."

"Well," says I, "if you're a cowman, why don't you get your cattle across that river?"

Then he told me all about the expert they had turned themselves over to.

"I'll cross your cattle," I said.

The first thing I did was to send back to our herd for four old cows that were used to swimming the Brazos. "That's all right," said the expert river man, who was by and had heard all that had passed. "That's right, put those cows in the lead, the steers will follow. I'll ride in a little above the herd and point 'em sorter down."

"No, by gosh," says I, "you'll stay right up there on the bank where you are, and if you wet a hair of your horse, you'd better expect to float a damned sight farther down Red River than you've ever been yet."

Well, to make a long story short, the expert kept clear of the water, the old cows took to the river as natural as alligators — especially when Duckworth put one of their calves in a skiff and pulled out with it for the other side — and in no time we had the cattle across. We put them over in two bunches, returning after the second bunch with the old cows that had proved so true in piloting over the first lot. Jim Taylor and I swam our mixed herd without a bobble.

Soon after the war ended, my brother Otho and I fixed up some picket pens at our old ranch north of Waco and began to road-brand herds from south Texas. We had complete equipment, including a long branding chute. It was a law, either written or unwritten, that after cattle crossed the Brazos they had to be road-branded. Of course, many of them were road-branded when they left the southern ranges, but many were not. Furthermore, it was to the owner's advantage to have fresh brands on his cattle when they reached such foreign ranges as the Indian Nation and Kansas. If they got away they could be more easily identified. Anything not road-branded was likely to be cut back at Red River.

Our proposition was to furnish hands and brand the cattle as directed by the owners. For big steers — and many from the lower country were from ten to fifteen years old — we charged 15 cents a head, and for everything under four years old 10 cents a head. In 1871 we road-branded more than four thousand head of cattle for the King Ranch alone. They came to us in four herds, and about the time we had one herd branded out the next would be on hand. It took five or six days to brand out one thousand steers.

It was while we were branding out a herd of these big King Ranch steers that I first saw a Mexican whip a steer. One rough old steer absolutely refused to go out of the big pen into the chute pen. He would fight men on horseback and dodge into corners. A Mexican working for us named Celi said, "You say so, me fight that steer and make him go into chute."

"Go to it," I told him.

Celi grabbed up a fence rail and made for the steer on foot. The steer ran at him; the Mexican dodged, and as the animal went by let him have a lick on the backbone that tamed him considerably. In no time Celi was right up on that steer's side prodding him into the chute.

But before a man undertook to deal afoot with one of these long-horned, maddened critters, he had better know his business. Once a herd of them stampeded right in Waco. Only a few houses were there then, and brush grew in the streets. A baker stepped out of his shop and shooed at one of the steers. The steer made a lunge at him and caught him under the chin with a horn, the point coming out of the man's mouth. The steer was a heavy, strong devil, and he dragged the baker for two hundred yards before a cowboy shot him. The baker died. The steer was butchered and the meat given away.

Once I saw a cowman drowned in the Brazos at Waco. The river was on a rise, and only after much trouble had the herd been crossed. The cowman could not swim, and he had kept his remuda of horses back to cross behind the cattle. His plan was to get a skiff, lead his horse, and let the other horses follow with some hands driving them. When all was ready, the men on shore gave the horse a scare to make him enter the water; the horse lunged so as to come down in the skiff with both forefeet. It turned over. The cowman had on boots, spurs, leggings, six-shooter and a money belt containing several hundred dollars. He went under and was not found until five days later.

Well, W. W. Burton swam his last river several years after I took down his talk. I think of him and his family often, and from the very memory get a better tonic than anything ever put in bottles.

Roy Bedichek

NATURE is the complex of all complexities. One part of a man may be as simple and serene as the cow chewing her cud in the noonday shade of a tree a thousand miles and a hundred years away from any milking machine; and yet the whole of this same man may be as complex as the genius of Shakespeare ever penetrated. It will be a great deal easier to show Roy Bedichek in the simplicities of naturalness than to express him in the naturalness of the highest intellectual and emotional complexities.

His going to bed with the chickens in summertime and not too much after them in the wintertime and getting up with the morning star at all times made his friends smile. He favored several kinds of independence common to the country. It did him good, he said, to walk out and empty his bladder on the ground instead of having to go in the house and empty it into a mechanical contrivance. I've heard him say that sometimes in the obscurity of before-daylight he would dig a hole in the ground out in the yard near "the shack" — his study — and excrete into it, covering the place with dirt like a cat. It gave him a satisfaction to fertilize the ground. He liked to cook outdoors, eat outdoors, sleep outdoors, look and listen outdoors, be at one with the unexplaining wind from the south, with the swing of the Great Dipper around the North Star, and with the first bobwhiting at dawn. He preferred camping on a hill so that he could watch the firmament, rather than down in a shady valley by water.

The last car he bought, in 1951, was a Dodge pickup truck in which he could carry enough water to make his camp on a hill comfortable for a day or two. This pickup was for camp purposes, but he used it to run about in also, his wife owning a sedan. He got an immense satisfaction out of trucking in cow manure, also occasionally chicken manure, for his compost pile, with which he annually fertilized his garden. He liked to haul his fireplace wood in from the country, especially cedar stumps so rotten at the base that they could be knocked over but otherwise sound and dry. He had complete camp equipment, including a tent-fly to go with the truck. Part of the equipment was a field guide to the flora of the country and a field guide to the birds. He always took along something to read as well as to consult; above all, he took along the most richly and variously stored mind I have known. Not for him the dream of retiring to some primitive land and mating with "some savage woman" to rear his "dusky race." For him back to nature was not back to the primitive.

His father, James Madison Bedichek, an ex-Confederate soldier, quoted philosophers and talked philosophy at the family dining table. He proved up on a quarter-section of land near the village of Eddy, not far from Waco in central Texas. Here he and his wife ran what they called the Eddy Scientific and Literary Institute, dubbed the Bedichek School by the public. Mrs. Bedichek boarded and roomed some of the pupils. Roy's aptitude for books was congenital. The atmosphere of literature and of thought was as natural to him as the atmosphere in which a lone buzzard soars over a cedar-covered hill or in which a coyote trots through the mesquite, sniffing for a woodrat's trail.

I would not call his taste exactly austere. He took pleasure in witty limericks, however bawdy. He could talk for hours with some cedar chopper whose literary vocabulary was limited to the printing on a bottle of Levi Garrett's snuff. I've heard him say a dozen times that he could no longer read American fiction because it is so pallid and insipid compared to the great Russian fiction rammed to the breech with vitality: Turgenev, Dostoevsky, Tolstoy. He admitted Balzac into their company. During a long span of his life he read the greater part of Shakespeare about once every two years. He developed the perspective and ripeness that can come only to an intelligence grounded in the humanities.

The Walt Whitman that he knew by heart and had absorbed into his very marrow was not the sentimentalized "good grey poet" but the tough poet of democracy. "He is our greatest exponent of Democracy among the poets," Bedi wrote me in a letter. " 'The reached hand, bringing up the laggards' — could there be a more expressive phrase of the true inwardness of Democracy than that?" His other favorite American writer was Thoreau, acid, with the wild taste, a rebel. Bedichek gloried in the influence that Thoreau's "Civil Disobedience" had on Gandhi and Gandhi's India and is still having over the world.

While he was writing *Adventures with a Texas Naturalist,* or maybe it was *Karankaway Country,* he made a habit of reading pages of Plato with his predawn coffee. Plato helped start the day for him on a noble plane and put him into a creative mood. At this time he would not wilt the freshest part of the day with the littlenesses and banalities of a morning newspaper. For no man writing a book has morning ever been, to quote a 1945 note from Bedichek, a time to "stoke the furnace of indignation against numerous manifestations of Fascism in this country." He never learned the Greek language, but his ideal of a balanced life, of a just proportion of the elements that make up a human being, was essentially Greek. In reading Homer, he compared several translations. As hundreds of quotations and allusions in his books and letters would show, the immortal essence of the Greeks was in his veins.

It seemed to me that the philosophy of Henry George had a more determining effect upon his economic views than any other writing. Henry George advocated a single tax and did not consider it just that an individual owner of real estate should collect the unearned increment given to it by population and labor. Bedichek believed in the single tax but would justify buying a piece of land by saying, "It's better to run with the hounds for your dinner than with the hare for your life."

Immanuel Kant's categorical imperative was his golden rule: Do only as you would have others do; or, act only as if you would have the act become universal law. The categorical imperative is contrary to the ways of greed and lust; so was Bedichek. He was as unenvying and as free from greed and jealousy as any man could be.

One time on Conversation Rock, at Austin's Barton Springs, where we swam daily, Fred Thompson was with us when I set out anathematizing the pasteurized, mogenized, vitaminized and otherwise bowdlerized n now sold in pasteboard cartons, this stuff having driv natural (raw) milk out of the market. I knew Bedi would respond.

When his children were young, he said, and Austin was still just a town, he kept two cows, staking them out on vacant lots near his home and milking them in a pen on his own premises. He "wanted the children to have clean, wholesome, natural milk." Now with gusto he demonstrated holding his head in a cow's flank while he milked, so that she could barely kick at all and could not go to pissing without conveying a warning through muscular contraction.

The last cow he had, he told us, about 1932 or 1933, was a four-gallon milker. She was very gentle and very much devoted to the Bedicheks, but keeping a cow and milking her became too much of a burden, and Bedi sold her to a man out near Deep Eddy on West Sixth Street. This man saw the cow being milked. Bedi told him that she wouldn't give milk unless she were treated gently and fed well. He got up at two o'clock in the morning to lead her to the purchaser, thus avoiding traffic. The purchaser had her not more than two or three days before he complained that the cow wasn't giving the milk claimed for her. He wanted his money back. Bedi went out there. The cow was shrunken and showed abuse. While the man was away for a minute, his wife told Bedi that her husband had beaten the cow. Bedi felt like beating the man, but he left. He didn't give him his money back, either. Anybody who knew him would as soon expect apples to fall up instead of down as for him to misrepresent a fact.

In the early 1920's he suffered from a rash caused, as he was told, from eating too much high-protein food, especially eggs. He became for the rest of his life what Sam Houston called "a damned vegetarian." He was not too rigid, however, to enjoy latitude upon occasion. As a guest he ate of the meat set before him. He took the lead many a time in getting a few men friends to go out in the country for a meal and talk. There was always a steak, and Bedi always insisted on cooking the steak over wood coals. Nobody could cook it better, and he was no slacker in eating his part of it. Cooking meat over an open fire in his mind mitigated any "protein poison" it might have; at a hotel table I've seen him dispose of an untouched steak to somebody else who could eat his own and another. He had a theory that the deeper down into the earth a plant puts its roots, the richer its fruit is. He positively gloated in dilating on the mineral and other virtues of pecans, since the tree has a long taproot. He loved to mix a green or a fruit salad and would linger long and lovingly in detailing his recipe.

In theory he was against doctors; I think he wrote considerably on a book intended to expose at least several sides of the medical profession — though he believed very much in his doctor daughter, Mary Virginia Carroll. He would quote an old proverb: "A man's either a fool or his own physician after forty." He said that a sick man should have as much sense as a sick cow: she quits eating and goes off and lies down.

Sometimes it didn't seem at all natural to me that Bedi should be practical. He was a productive gardener, as his table, his deep-freeze, and many a mess of vegetables he gave to friends showed. Yet he put a kind of ritualism into gardening that farmer folks wouldn't and couldn't bother with. When I rode with him in his pickup I constantly wondered how he made it through the streets.

In the vigor of early manhood Bedi drank some whiskey — maybe not too much — although after he married, any drinking was bad economically. I don't think he ever loved any man quite so much as he loved his college friend Harry Steger, with whom he bicycled through Europe and who died young. He cried all day long, so Mrs. Bedichek has told me, after receiving word of Steger's death. One of his favorite anecdotes was of meeting Steger on Congress Avenue in Austin one day. They both wanted a drink but before entering a saloon swore to each other that they would take only one and then get out. They took the drink, and it was good. "Well, let's go," said Bedi. "That drink makes me feel like a new man," Steger said, "and now the new man has to have a drink." I never did ask Bedi if he joined the new man.

By the time I got to know him, he wasn't smoking the pipe or cigar he had once smoked. He took real solace in a bottle of beer along in the evening or with Mexican food — but virtually never more than one. Along about 1954 or 1955 in the middle of a terrible drouth devastating much of Texas, I brought back about a dozen cases of Carta Blanca beer from Monterrey, Mexico. I had a devil of a time getting them past the customs ignoramuses at Laredo. I had to prove my right to pay duty on beer just as beer dealers pay it. I hadn't more than reached Austin and got a few bottles cooled than I called up Bedi. For a while I shared that Carta Blanca beer with other people, especially when Bedi was around. When only two cases were left, I cut off everybody, including myself, and saved it for Bedichek. Occasionally there might be two or three or half a dozen other men; I'd offer them what they wanted to drink, and if they wanted beer they had to take Schlitz (Bedi's second choice) or something else. Then I'd bring out Bedi's bottle of Carta Blanca. He enjoyed that sort of petting.

As newspaperman, chamber of commerce exponent, and director of the Interscholastic League of Texas, Bedichek had done a vast amount of hackwork. Anybody who works for a living spends most of his energies in hackwork. But though he was a university man, specializing in the humanities, he had never been deflected by the Ph.D. system into inferior literature. He had spent a lifetime reading the best before he turned author with seventy just over the hill for him. While H. Y. Benedict was president of the University of Texas, I heard him say that Bedichek should be teaching literature. "Why not put him to teaching it?" I asked. "Because every Ph.D. professor of English would have a colt if I did," he replied. That was the truth! Sawdust never yearns toward vitality.

We all learn with wonder of the feats of memory performed by the Macaulays of history, but I've never known anyone else in the flesh who held in memory so precisely so much of what he had read as Roy Bedichek. He could have produced a magnificent anthology of English poetry solely out of his memory — as rich as that Lord Wavell drew from his memory in *Other Men's Flowers*. He had the added faculty, perhaps of a higher order, of always being able to draw from memory anything related to a subject brought up by conversation or in his own flow of thought. Sometimes he had to restrain himself from clogging his writing with allusions and "decisions that had from the time of King William come down."

Early in the summer of 1953 Jess Akin of Austin decided to paint the portraits of Bedichek, Walter Webb, and myself. He had painted mine unsatisfactorily and wanted to make another attempt. If a person is being portrayed for his significance, every effort should be made to make that significance appear on his countenance while he is sitting for the painter. I volunteered to do my best to keep Bedi's features illuminated while he was being painted. I knew that he would do more talking than I, for he was just naturally a better talker. I illuminated him for four half-days. After Akin was through with Bedi, he took me on, and Bedi came to brighten me. We had eight conversations amounting to perhaps thirty hours in less than two weeks. I can say of Bedichek as Johnson said of Burke, "That man draws out all my powers." Neither he nor I was empty or exhausted when the sittings came to an end.

Sitting and talking had become a kind of occupation with us. Several times I thought I would make notes on the subjects of our talk. I did not. Naturally, we returned occasionally to the same themes — but without repeating. Now I cannot recall a hundredth part of what either said; if I could recall all, a book would be required to hold it. Little of it was trivial. It interested us, and that was sufficient. Bedi's mind played on any subject brought up — from fleas to Plato. I never forget his quoting the cowboy who said he didn't mind so much what the fleas ate as their tromping around.

Will Burges, lawyer of El Paso, John Lomax of cowboy song fame, and Roy Bedichek were the pithiest and vividest relators of anecdotes about human beings they had encountered that I have known. Despite his rich stores out of books, Bedichek in the course of conversations with his peers drew more often from actual experience. He could make any character that interested him fascinating. He told few stories except to reveal character, to bring out some point, or to complement something else. Lots of times one merry tale would call up another.

Boswell's life of Johnson is the greatest biography in the world because it records the best talk that has ever been recorded. Bedichek often talked as well as Johnson talked — but he had no Boswell to record more than a few snatches of what he said.

One day he and I were talking about the influence of sounds on human character. Suppose, we speculated, two brothers of equal endowments by nature were separated at an early age and one was placed where all the sounds he heard were harmonies and the other was placed where he had to listen day and night to harsh, metallic, often idiotic disharmonies. What would be the differences in them after they had absorbed until maturity these sounds so opposing in quality?

After talking on this and other subjects for about two hours, we repaired to a tavern for refreshments.

"It's as quiet here as in a civilized English pub," I said.

"Just wait," Bedi said.

Not more than three minutes passed before a cross between a drool and a squawk began to volume out of a wall vent right over us. Some person of barbaric taste and ear had put a nickel into the nickelodeon. We shifted to another table, but the pleasantness of the atmosphere had been shattered. Presumably the landlord was happy over his percentage of the nickelodeon intake.

Bedi remembered how at Barton Springs we used to lie on the warm rocks and listen to the wind talking in the cottonwoods, and how now we try to rule out of our ears the hideous sounds coming through a loudspeaker attached to a coin-hungry machine. I told Bedi that the sounds called up Joseph Conrad's epithet for the music at a honky-tonk: "murder of silence."

" 'Murder of silence' is good," he said. "It is the murder also of peace and of just thinking."

As president of the Texas Institute of Letters, I had notice from judges of books published during the year 1956 that Bedichek had won the Carr P. Collins $1,000 award, to be presented at the Institute's annual dinner in Dallas, February 1, 1957. On the evening of January 20, I went to his home, finding him alone. I had telephoned him that I had a letter to confront him with. He was eating a salad of tomatoes, lettuce, cheese, and a little mayonnaise, moistening it down with a glass of buttermilk. He thought I should take a little something and spooned out yogurt into a bowl and put honey on it. We were both honey hounds, honey being the highest form of sweetness — natural. I could not remember having tasted yogurt before. He told me how monks in a Hungarian monastery had cultivated the yogurt germ hundreds of years ago, keeping it secret; how one escaped with the process to Canada, whence it came to California, where yogurt is now made and sold. "I get the yeast in a container every three weeks by air mail," Bedi said, "and make six quarts." He described in detail the sanitary processes for making yogurt and its bodily virtues. "Not the same thing at all," he said, "that you buy in grocery stores." I found it delicious.

After the yogurt, I confronted him with the letter. He read it aloud slowly. When he came to the point — the $1,000 award to Roy Bedichek for his book *Educational Competition* — he stopped, joy on his face. We talked a little and then he said, "Dobie, you'll go away and I'll think that I dreamed you were here with this announcement.

"About three thousand years ago a disciple of a Chinese philosopher named Chuang-tzu came to him one morning and said, 'Master, I dreamed last night that I was a butterfly.' The philosopher looked at him hard and said, 'Sir, are you sure now that you are not a butterfly dreaming that you are a man?'

"That word *confront* you used over the telephone had me puzzled," Bedi continued. "You are somewhat of a precisionist, and *confront* bears the connotation of something unpleasant. I was wondering what sort of blackguard had been denouncing me or what you could have against me."

Thousands of words had special connotations for him. About the time I carried the good news of the $1,000 prize, the secretary of the Town and Gown Club, to which we both belonged, sent out an announcement of a paper to be read by Bedichek at the fortnightly dinner. His subject was "Water and Soil Conservation in Texas." I noticed the use of that word "confront" in a quotation from Bedi on what he was going to say:

"That which I shall write will be down — I fear far down — on the lay level. The authorities bristle with statistics which I only vaguely understand and speak in a jargon that I don't savvy except in spots. Hence my modesty may be compared to that of the Negro in the folk rhyme who was confronted with a medical emergency:

> *'Ah ain't no doctor nor no doctor's son*
> *But Ah kin hol' de patient till de doctor come.'* "

I shall die regretting that I did not set down on paper a thousand passages of Bedichek talk before they faded from my mind. Here is a brief note I typed on the night of September 6, 1957. It illustrates the mobility, and homeliness too, characteristic of Bedichek's mind.

Bill Owens, writer and teacher in Columbia University, New York, and Bedichek's friend, came to town, and this evening after a swim we sat down under the big elm in our backyard to drink beer and talk. When I brought out three cans in two hands, Bedi told this story, which, he said, came to him from an income-tax man.

In Minnesota, it seems, there is some kind of income-tax law whereby a higher percentage is charged on income made by a joint furnishing entertainment with beer than from one that does not furnish it. Anyhow, a Swedish woman opened up a beer tavern in Minnesota and it was soon notorious for the patronage it drew. A tax man went to inspect it.

He saw the place crowded with men. There were other beer places not far away with only small crowds. All sold the same beer. What was the attraction here? The inspector could see no dance girls, no entertainer of any kind, not even a television set. Then he saw the proprietress emerging from behind the counter carrying four bottles of beer. She had one in each hand and one sitting on each breast, where they stood steady while she moved with energy and she did not touch them. Was this entertainment?

I heard Bedichek tell the story that follows more than once, each time with a gusto of distaste. At a big dinner provided by public-spirited women for the male pillars of society in their town, Bedichek sat opposite an especially large pillar. The man took two and three helpings of everything that came along. Dessert was a piece of cake with a small dish of strawberries. After it had been placed in front of each diner and some were already eating, a lady began passing a bowl of whipped cream to go on the strawberries. By the time the bowl got to the large pillar in front of Bedichek he had consumed his strawberries and cake. He did not look up or to the right or to the left while he ate. He looked down, eating with his eyes as well as with his jowls and gullet. When the big bowl of whipped cream came in front of him, he accepted it as an addition to what he had evidently considered a too meager dessert. He began ladling the whipped cream out of the bowl into his mouth and did not cease ladling until there was nothing left to ladle. He even scraped the sides and bottom of the bowl. Then he looked up and wiped his mouth, put his hands on his stomach and said, "That goes pretty good."

I keep referring to talk at Barton Springs. One day while we were sunning after a dip in the cold water, Bedi remarked that a "farm-type of woman" he had encountered that morning reminded him of a wise old mare.

"After an old mare has had eight to ten colts," he said, "she gets a look of wisdom hardly seen in the eyes of the wisest philosopher."

On August 7, 1957, after a cold, cold swim in Barton

Springs, we sat down about dusk to double hotness in a Mexican restaurant. This is one of the few uses of the word "Mexican" remaining active. Mexican restaurants in Texas are no longer run by Mexicans but by Latin-Americans. With Bedichek and me was our younger friend Wilson Hudson.

Bedichek told this story:

One time out in Amarillo they were having a prohibition election. The pros imported a high-powered speaker to convert the heathen and packed the biggest gathering place in town with an audience. This speaker quoted poetry and displayed all sorts of diagrams showing the effects of alcohol on the human organs. Then he unrolled a long linen chart and hung it up on the wall to demonstrate the waste of money on alcohol. The figures and letters on this chart were boxcar size so that they could be read half a block away.

But the speaker was adding emphasis by reading them out in a loud voice. Up at the top were so many millions and billions spent each year in America for food, so many for clothes, so many on churches, so many on education, and on through the catalogue. The figures were soaring and the speaker's voice soared to a climax as he read out the billions spent on whiskey.

"And, by God, it's worth it," a mighty voice rang out. It was the voice of Buttermilk Jones. The announcement of his sense of values came in a way that absolutely killed the speaker's facts and figures.

"Why," Wilson Hudson now asked, "did they call him Buttermilk Jones?"

"Because he never drank buttermilk, I guess," Bedi answered.

"This putting a high value on whiskey makes me

think of an incident during prohibition days," I said. "Not long after the end of World War I, an Englishman and a Texan were partners trading in oil leases and royalties out in the Burkburnett Field. Some bootleggers were making more than owners of oil wells. One day a big well came in on land controlled by the partners; within fifteen minutes they cleared a hundred thousand dollars by selling a fraction of what they owned, and they decided right there to celebrate the occasion.

"The Englishman rustled around and found a fifth of Canadian Club whiskey for sale at fifty dollars. He bought it and took it to their room. He opened it and poured the contents over ice. Raising his glass, he said, 'Here's to whiskey! — the only time in my life I ever paid what it's worth.' "

Two evenings after this — and a lot of other — talk, we three met again, this time on a shady lawn. I read aloud what I had written, received a few corrections, and saw about three dozen words, sentence structures, and idea combinations to work on. Two evenings later we met again, in a darkening, air-conditioned room, fresh again from Barton Springs with fresh thirst. As we were raising our beer cans, Bedi quoted:

> *A chield's amang you takin' notes,*
> *And faith he'll prent it.*

I despair at getting into print the felicity and fitness with which Bedichek was forever drawing out of his storehouse. Many writers, perhaps most, read in order to suck in something that they can feed out. During most of his life Bedi read to delight and enlarge his own mind. Now how in the devil had he come to remember those lines from Burns's "On the Late Captain Grose's

Peregrinations Thro' Scotland"? (He had to tell me the source.) And how in the devil could they lie down there in the cellar of his memory for a generation or two and then, just as occasion arose for their application, jump to the surface like an empty corked bottle released at the bottom of a pool?

On February 24, 1957, I paid Bedi a visit in his shack, taking with me for him a paperbound copy of A. E. Taylor's *Socrates, the Man and His Thought*. On the flyleaf I had written:

Dear Bedi,

I give you this book because I would be as bereft if you went away as Crito and the others were when Socrates went. As one of them said of him, I can say of you, my friend, "the wisest and justest and best man that I have ever known."

— Dobie, 24 February 1957.

Two days later I received this letter:

Dear, dear Dobie —

After I had been about an hour at work this morning I glanced up and saw the volume *Socrates* you gave me yesterday. I remembered that I had seen some writing on the flyleaf which I didn't take time to read while you were here. I had dismissed it momentarily as a "good wishes" inscription and so had let it escape my attention.

I reached up and got the volume in my hand "just to see." I was affected to tears, and I don't mean metaphorical tears but a real secretion from the lachrymose glands. One got loose from the inner corner of my left eye and it felt wet and warm, so I know they were real.

The old Greeks (bless them) were not ashamed of tears. That shame was a part of the sentimentalism and masculine assumption of superiority of that romanticism which assigned tears to women. I am profoundly affected, (stirred emotionally in that nervous plexus situated in the abdomen) by your placing me in a unique position in your affections. Truly, I have felt towards you a friendship I never felt for anyone else except for Harry Steger, who died 44 years ago.

Bless you for recording this where I can turn to it when sometimes "the world is dark and I a wanderer who has lost his way."

Yours,

February 25, 1957   Bedi

Two or three years before this, standing in a group of friends, I said to Bedi, "You are as good as grass."

"Don Quixote," he said, "once told Sancho Panza, 'You are as good as bread. Nothing but the sexton and his spade will ever part us.' "

The sexton and his spade came shortly before noon of May 21, 1959. Bedichek, after working all morning in his study out in the yard, his "shack," came into the kitchen and asked his wife how soon lunch would be ready. He wanted time after lunch for a nap before starting out in his pickup with Wilson Hudson and me to Paisano, my place on Barton Creek, to bring back cedar stumps for winter burning.

"It's ready now except the cornbread and it's baking," Mrs. Bedichek said.

"I'll wait for it," he replied and sat down. These were his last words.

When Rodney Kidd comes to see me, I am apt to pump him. In the Texas Interscholastic League he knew Roy Bedichek better than many scholars know their books. What follows is a construction of notes made on Kidd's talk.

At one time Bedichek proposed that he and Rodney Kidd prepare a guide to Texas camping, confining the camps mostly to places open to the public and naming the flowers and birds to be seen about the campsites at different times of the year. The western itinerary was to start at Buchanan Lake on the Colorado River above Austin, go on west to Brownwood Lake, thence to a lake near Breckenridge, then to Vernon and Wichita Falls and a lake on one of the streams of the region.

In Vernon they met Robert Anderson, manager of the Waggoner Estate, who became Secretary of the Treasury under Eisenhower. I quote Rodney Kidd: "He told us where he wanted us to stay all night, then took us to a luxurious place and pointed out the room Mr. Bedichek was to stay in. 'Rodney, you can stay here,' he said. 'Here's the kitchen.' He opened an icebox with everything in it.

"Mr. Bedichek said, 'Well, I'll tell you, Bob, Kidd and I have settled on a prettier place than this.'

"Bob's eyes sort of bugged. 'Why,' he said, 'I consider this a mighty nice spot. I don't think you can find a nicer one for either looks or comfort.'

" 'Oh, yes we can — over yonder on that lake,' Bedichek answered.

" 'Are you all going to sleep out tonight?' Anderson asked.

" 'We sleep out every night.'

"Near Canadian, out in the sandhills, we found a beautiful lake that the federal government had built. A native warned us against coons, said we'd better lock up at night. 'These coons will eat up everything you've got,' he said. 'They'll get in your car; they'll get in the grub boxes.' The next morning we found where they'd been after everything we had. The plentiful deer and birds were not so acquisitive.

"One time we turned north from Rio Grande City on a country road that led to Hebbronville. We went by an old adobe house, the walls barely standing, some Mexicans living in a part of the building. They had a kind of store. Mr. Bedichek said, 'Let's go in and see what we can see.' We couldn't speak Mexican, and they couldn't speak English. Through the mesquite brush I could see the remains of an abandoned ranch house. I went over there and found an old handmade Spanish bedstead, walnut. Bedi and I camped there for the night.

"The next morning we heard knocking going on — knock-knock. We couldn't imagine what it was. It was springtime. We took out to investigate and came upon two big land terrapins clashing against each other. As we stood watching, Mr. Bedichek said, "Isn't that a hell of a thing?' He made notes on the behavior of the hardshell terrapins. Two males were fighting over a female, off to one side. Each was trying to turn the other one over. When a terrapin gets planted on his back, he's had it, you know. There is no way for a hardshell terrapin so placed to regain his position. Finally one of the contenders succeeded. There the victim lay helpless on his back with his feet up in the air.

"The victor went off with the female. Mr. Bedichek said, 'Well, that's nature. That boy won his battle fair and square. Let him go.' Bedi would not touch the victim. 'His position is according to nature,' Bedi said. 'A hawk's catching a crippled bird keeps the balance in nature. That is necessary in a natural world.'

"One time while we were camped on a creek we heard a frog giving repeated sounds of distress. We went down and saw that a water moccasin had the rear end of the frog in his grip. The frog could holler until the moccasin swallowed him. According to the Bedichek philosophy, here again nature was taking its course, merely maintaining the balance."

One year in their capacities as director of the University Interscholastic League and assistant, Bedichek and Kidd were obliged to go to Lufkin over in east Texas to make an investigation. Bedichek stocked his portable icebox with materials for supper, including two cans of Schlitz beer, cheese, lightbread, quantities of lettuce, carrots, tomatoes and other "rabbit food," but no meat. They ate an early supper off the road and drove into the town of Trinity to spend the night, within easy reach of Lufkin.

As Rodney Kidd relates, they "found an old, two-story frame hotel, just across the street from the depot. The landlady was congenial and eager for customers. Apparently she did not have many; her hotel lacked modern conveniences. With pride she led us upstairs to a large front room fitted with two big double beds. Mr. Bedichek observed the railroad tracks and considered the noise freight trains make. We could not, he said, possibly sleep in the same room because he snored so loudly. He would have to be quartered in a separate room.

"The landlady showed him another big room, on the back side of the house; this was just to his liking. In one corner a washstand held a crock washbowl with an old-time pitcher full of water sitting inside it. A drop-light furnished with a 50-watt bulb hung from the center of the ceiling. The room would be absolutely quiet, the landlady assured Mr. Bedichek. She knew, for her own bedroom was immediately underneath, and it was always quiet.

"To an inquiry, he informed her that he did not eat breakfast, although he was sure his friend would be interested. I assumed that he was against eating breakfast in such an old hotel and wanted to make, as usual, his own coffee. However, he did not tell the landlady that he was going to make coffee in his room. He was afraid she would not approve.

"After she had gone and he had brought in his things, his next task was to hook up his coffee-making arrangements. I helped him move the center table to a spot directly under the single droplight. Then he got out his hot plate, his small coffeepot and the small boiler in which he heated water. He measured water out of the pitcher and placed it in the boiler, then measured the coffee and placed it in the top of the dripolator. Everything was now in readiness for him to make coffee without disturbing anyone. He always took great pains with brewing coffee and actually considered himself the greatest coffee maker in the country.

"He planned to get up about 4 A.M., as was his custom, plug in his hot plate, drink his coffee, read Plato or Aristotle or Socrates until daylight and then step out and view the birds.

"Next morning I woke up fairly early, dressed, and went down to a fine breakfast. Not a word did I hear from Mr. Bedichek. The landlady reported that she had heard some commotion a good while before daylight but had heard nothing since. I wondered whether he was well and, being a little worried, went as soon as I had finished my breakfast to see what had happened. By this hour he was always about with fieldglasses in hand. Opening the door to his room, I found him propped up in bed, reading but not, apparently, in a happy humor. 'Chief,' I asked, 'what in the world has happened? Are you all right?' I had observed a little heap of soiled clothing near the bed.

"He proceeded to relate, in detail, the events of the night. At 4 A.M. he had got up and, in order to plug in his hot plate and boil water for coffee, had disconnected the light bulb, put in the socket connected with the hot plate, and when the water boiled, poured it into the dripolator. Then, while his coffee dripped, he had decided to put the light bulb back in so that he could read and drink his coffee in desirable leisure. Moving about to disconnect the hot plate, his elbow had caught in the cord, the coffeepot had turned over in the middle of the floor, and there he was. Immediately he remembered that the old biddy was sleeping directly under his room. He was afraid that the hot coffee would run through cracks in the floor and drip down on her in bed. It was still dark. When he reached for something to mop with, he picked up the first rag he felt. Hastily he mopped the floor. After taking care of the emergency, he proceeded to reconnect the light bulb.

"Then he discovered that the coffeepot had spilled over his shoes and socks and that he had used his shirt and underclothes to mop with. Not only had he lost his coffee but he had ruined his shirt. He had coffee grounds in his shoes and he had not had any breakfast.

" 'Kidd, what did you have for breakfast?' he asked.

" 'Chief, you did not miss much.'

" 'I thought that was about the way it would be.' Mr. Bedichek was pleased to have his anticipated judgment verified.

"Then I continued, 'All I had was some light, fluffy, hot, brown biscuits. And you know I don't like butter. I have got used to oleomargarine. These biscuits had fresh country butter to put on them and blackberry jam. I am positive it was homemade. I don't know if you would like it, but I found it mighty tasty. The old lady is an excellent coffee maker, too. And she had big country eggs, the kind that stand up in the plate when fried, no penthouse stuff out of your battery-fed chickens.'

" 'Hell, Kidd, don't tell me any more. Take this $5 and go down to the store and get me another shirt, a pair of socks and a pair of shorts, so that we can get on with the Lufkin investigation.' "

Walter Prescott Webb

WALTER Prescott Webb and I were born in the same year, 1888. He belonged to one drouth-scarred part of Texas, I to another. His father was a country schoolteacher who homesteaded a quarter-section of poor land; mine was a rancher who hoped that education would lead his sons to a better occupation. Webb came to the University of Texas as instructor in history in 1918, while I was a soldier in France, four years after I had come as instructor in English. We advanced concurrently, along divergent ways, as underlings at the University.

Our friendship developed more after about 1930, it seems to me, but I was never close to him as I was with Roy Bedichek, the dearest comrade of my life. Webb had sides never revealed directly to me. As writers and men, Bedichek, Webb, and Dobie have been linked together — mostly by Texas people — many times in speech and in print.

Bedichek was a kind of peg on which my happiest associations with Webb hung. For years we three sat together, with other men, at the same table during fortnightly dinners, "papers," and discussions of the Town and Gown Club of Austin, but talk at our table was seldom so free and personal as it always was at prolonged picnic suppers in the country. Bedichek was the habitual planner of these supper parties, also cooker of the steaks. The earliest of these picnic suppers that I remember were not far beyond the Rob Roy Ranch, some distance off the Bee Caves road in the hills west of Austin. Bedi liked to camp high up. At one hilltop camp we looked down on bullbats (nighthawks) booming as they dived for insects. After Webb, in 1942, acquired Friday Mountain Ranch, about seventeen miles southwest of Austin, a location there on Bear Creek became our supping and conversation grounds, though in the fifties we went several times to a place I owned in Burnet County named Cherry Springs — on account of wild cherry trees growing by Fall Creek.

I would take potato salad prepared by Bertha Dobie as nobody else could prepare it. Someone might take something else; Bedichek brought steaks, bread, tomatoes, lettuce, beer, and so on, and then saw that each man paid his share. Nobody was host and the drinking was moderate — one can of beer for Bedi. Webb did not really care for any. When he took whiskey, on other occasions, a jigger without water would do him all evening. He had not drunk at all until he was about fifty. Sitting with the dons after dinner at his college — Queen's in Oxford, where he was Harmsworth Professor of American History during 1942–1943 — he had developed a mild taste for wine. He craved coffee. Bedichek was particular in boiling coffee, which he furnished, along with pot, tin plates, knives, and forks.

Mody Boatright and Wilson Hudson, both of the University of Texas English department, were regulars at these campfire suppers. After Frank Wardlaw came as director of the University Press, he added to talk and geniality. Any time that John Henry Faulk or Glen Evans was in town, he was there. One time, during World War II, Faulk brought an Englishman along, and in capping limericks with each other both proved themselves bottomless artesian wells. I remember Coke Stevenson, then governor, saying at one supper — the only one he attended — that the American frontiersman carried a rifle, an ax, and a Bible. This was at Friday Mountain. We were by the same water when Homer Price Rainey, president of the University, told us that the regents were out to gut him. Ours was no club in any organized way, and we never had regular gatherings, but all of us were liberal enough to be for Rainey and against the reactionary regents who for several years dominated the University of Texas.

While dismissing Rainey, the regents, in October, 1944, elected Dr. T. S. Painter acting president. Immediately thereafter he said in a letter addressed to the faculty: "I want it definitely understood that I am not a candidate for the position of permanent president, and I would not accept it if it were offered to me." The regents wanted an agent. Before long it was clear that they had what they wanted. When, in May, 1946, they elected Painter president and he accepted the offer, a caucus of faculty men asked Webb to formulate their opinions. At a special meeting of the faculty a few days later Webb countered a resolution "assuring President Painter of our support and cooperation" with one expressing "deep regret that Dr. Painter has not reciprocated the trust the faculty reposed in him, but has, on the contrary, broken faith and violated his pledge." The Webb motion of disconfidence failed to carry by a vote of 160 to 186.

Few other men of his stature and intellectual power have experienced so intimately the choke of poverty. This is why he helped so generously many a student with brains but without adequate financial resources. He cherished privately Hans Christian Andersen's story "The Ugly Duckling," and gave copies to students battling against odds.

As prosperity made him aware of the independence that it gives to an individual, he became, it seems to me, more actively considerate of that basis of freedom for other individuals and for Texas and the South.

His *Divided We Stand* (1937) was a stand for fairness. Based on figures in *The World Almanac* and the United States census, it made out a case against the prospering North for keeping the South in poverty as a colonial dependent until Franklin D. Roosevelt and the New Deal reversed the trend. Later Webb made clear that vast oil fields and rising industrialism in the South resulting from World War II advanced the region's prosperity.

In his later years Webb drew a good salary as a distinguished professor. Beyond salaries (and motion picture rights amounting to $10,000 on his book *The Texas Rangers*), he prospered through investing earnings from teaching and writing — especially from two textbooks — in real estate. A few years ago he drew up a plan to enable faculty members of the University of Texas who so wished and who had the money to invest in real estate. This plan, as far as I know, never got into operation.

Several times I heard him speak of the influence of

L. M. Keasbey on his life. Before World War I, Keasbey, a professor in the University, gave a course on economics — though it was entitled "institutional history" — in which he emphasized one way to get rich: invest in land that the activities of an increasing population will make more valuable, very valuable if the land be chosen judiciously. At the time Webb was absorbing directions to the "unearned increment," an Austin peddler and then wholesale shipper of vegetables named M. H. Crockett took the Keasbey course. He, as I observed and as I heard him tell with pride, became expert in anticipating traffic routes of the city; he died one of the richest property owners in it.

Webb wrote little on civil rights. A few years after the decision of the Supreme Court of the United States desegregating public schools, he could write and speak on the South's advancing economic prosperity without touching on the Negro. Yet he did not ignore the subject. In a paper to have been delivered at Rice University shortly after he died, he said: "The Southerner is so concerned with the racial issue that he has no time for anything else. This is the foremost issue that has plagued the South since 1820 . . . . The racial issue is too heavy to move; it is too green to burn; the best we can do for the present is to plow around it and cultivate the rest of the field."

Friday Mountain Ranch consists of approximately a section of land that was, when Webb acquired it, eroded, devoid of humus, bare of vegetation beyond cedars on the hills and broomweeds in the valley. He had wastage accumulated at the cotton gins east of Austin hauled out to spread on the ground. He applied commercial fertilizer to plots no longer tillable. While he was Harmsworth Professor of American History at Oxford University, he gave his address to the English *Who's Who* as Friday Mountain Ranch, Austin, Texas. He belonged to it. During the terrible drouth that began late in the forties and did not end until 1957 he made slow progress in restoring the soil and growing a turf of grass — a turf that reached its climax the spring he died.

He figured that the land would someday pay for the expenses he had been out on it. It did, by increase of real estate prices. Beyond all, he valued and enjoyed grass for itself, beautiful on any land, the mark of bounty on ground once impoverished. Several times when I was with him where grass flourished I saw him gather seeds of sideoats grama, little bluestem, Indian grass, and switch grass to take to Friday Mountain and scatter around. In planning near the end of his life to transfer title to the land, he chose as purchaser a friend, Rodney Kidd, who would maintain the turf.

He was not a naturalist in the way that Bedichek was, but he observed. Twice at least he told me that we had missed much out of life by not learning botany while growing up in the country. One time, as four or five of us were riding in a car along Fall Creek in Burnet County, he called out to halt. He had spotted a hackberry, about twenty feet high, growing up through the hollow trunk of a big dead live oak. He did not swim, but the pools of water impounded by dams he had constructed across Bear Creek gave him as much pleasure as any swimming hole ever gave any swimmer.

His brief book *Flat Top: A Story of Modern Ranching,* printed and published by Carl Hertzog of El Paso in 1960, is on grass and a man of grass named Charles Pettit. In 1938 Mr. Pettit bought 7,000 acres, to which he added 10,000 acres of worn-out, eroded farms. Year after year he combated weeds, prickly pear, and other competitors of grass. Year after year he applied ferti-lizer, planted clover, put out seeds of native grasses. He impounded over 3,400 acre-feet of water, brought back a turf of grasses waist-high. After living with the land for a quarter of a century, he made the ranch pay. "The man really loves grass," Webb wrote. If Webb also had not loved grass, he would never have written this ac-count of a model ranch in conservation practices.

About the time I was leaving for England late in 1945 to teach at Shrivenham, in a G.I. university, a civilized man of wealth who demanded anonymity granted a sum of money to relieve Roy Bedichek for a year from his duties as director of the Interscholastic League of Texas. He had a book to write. Webb invited him to take over a big upstairs room with a fireplace in the old Friday Mountain rock house, which had originally been built for a boys' academy. Here, eager in his liberation, Bedichek made shelves of apple boxes to hold his books, carried water by bucket from an old dug well, brought up wood, cooked over the open fire. Through the year 1956 he worked at a table in front of the fireplace.

Chickens mechanically grown in rooms downstairs did not bother him. In fact, he based one of his richest chapters on "Denatured Chickens." Associating with him-self, letting his richly stored mind play, adding meanings to long-accumulating observations on people, birds, wild flowers, trees, and other forms of life, he achieved *Ad-ventures with a Texas Naturalist*. Published in 1947, it was fourteen years later taken over by the University of Texas Press, an institution that Webb, more than any other man in the faculty, had furthered. "The Bedichek

Room" remains through Webb and Rodney Kidd a feature at Friday Mountain.

Webb's *The Great Frontier,* officially published December 8, 1952, won the Carr P. Collins Award of $1,000 given annually by the Texas Institute of Letters. His response to the presentation was the after-dinner address to the Institute — and mighty fidgety he was before dinner. He asked me, also others, to notice how people received what he had to say, something so intimate to him that he shrank from making it public. He read his say. It was the most moving I have heard any man utter. He waited a long time to publish it, with some added details, under title of "The search for William E. Hinds," in *Harper's* magazine, July, 1961. *Reader's Digest* published a condensation of it the following month.

The subject of autobiography came up several times among us while Bedichek was still on hand, iterating that he lacked the genius of Jean-Jacques Rousseau for confession. As Webb was leaving my house one day in 1960, I again spoke about autobiography. He volunteered that he had written one while at Oxford University, 1942–1943. He did not go into detail. The whole cannot, I believe, have anything else so intensely, so poignantly personal as the chapter in which he tells of a response received in 1904 to a letter he had written to the letter column of the *Sunny South.* It was from William E. Hinds of New York, an utter stranger, not only commending his ambition to be a writer but offering to send him books and magazines. Later this William E. Hinds urged him to get a college education and loaned him money while he was attending the University of

Texas. Hinds died 45 years before Webb's obligation to him became a chapter in published literature.

It resulted in many letters from unknowns, some sending money to help students as Hinds had helped Webb. For years he had been concerned over some way to requite Hinds and had given financial aid to able but needy students. He now set up the William E. Hinds scholarship fund at the University of Texas. After his death a check donating money to it was found in his pocketbook; it is an ultimate beneficiary in his will. The Hinds-Webb Scholarship Fund is now the official name.

I have no recollection of having heard Webb speak at any time of his soul, his religion, or God. He belonged to no church, ignored churches, liked some freethinkers, some churchmen, especially Dr. Edmund Heinsohn, long pastor of the University Methodist Church in Austin. After Heinsohn became a member of Town and Gown years ago, he often sat with Bedichek, Webb, and Dobie. He conducted Bedichek's funeral services, reading into them an interpretation of the man's character. At Webb's funeral he read an interpretive sketch of Webb's life. "I remain an agnostic," Somerset Maugham wrote in *The Summing Up,* "and the practical outcome of agnosticism is that you act as though God did not exist." As far as I can see, Walter Webb's positive goodness bore no relation to what is called God. His conduct was not determined by biblical injunctions or by expectation of reward in some sort of post-mortem existence. His mother is said to have been a fundamentalist, his father a skeptic who read the Bible in order to refute more specifically some of her credulities.

I cannot imagine Webb's "praying for guidance," but at one time he believed in something beyond. After he married in 1916 he was teaching in San Antonio and became so low-spirited over the future that he, as I recall his story, was about to take a job in a jewelry store. He consulted a noted fortune-teller known as Madam Skirls. She said, "The child will be a girl. I see nothing but books." With books he continued.

If the radical right appeared unjust and undemocratic to him, the radical left increasingly annoyed him. He was not a crusader and was not contentious. He sometimes wished, he once told me, that he did not have to think. He hungered after brightness and cheerful talk. His sense of humor tended to progress from anecdotes of rusticity to sharp wit. He loved stories, especially of people, and told them well. Often they were ironic or satiric. Webb's article "How the Republican Party Lost Its Future," from the *Southwest Review,* Autumn, 1949, ends with this story: "Their plight [that of the Republican Party] is like that of the man who had spent his life preparing for the future. It was his obsession. He awoke one morning on his birthday and began to appraise himself, his age which was considerable, his hair which had grown thin, his muscles a little flabby now, and his bones which seemed to have sand grains in the joints. After some contemplation, he struck his hand to his head and exclaimed, 'Heavens! This *is* my future!' "

He held — at one time, at least — that a certain strengthening of the mind comes through playing poker. He liked to play poker and played with skill.

One time while he and I were walking along the railroad about Third Street in Austin, we stopped beside an old-time locomotive, stationary, throbbing with power.

Webb said, "That is the greatest manifestation of power in the world." I told him that out of respect for its symbolism of power, Dr. Sanders, professor of Latin and Greek at Southwestern University about the beginning of the century, would remove his hat in salute to a steam engine pulling a train past him.

Whether Webb actually ever hated anybody I cannot say. I never heard him express hatred of any kind. He could be caustic, as when he wished that birth control had been in practice before a certain individual was born. He was more likely to set forth the facts about a man than to praise or condemn. He inclined to the policy of Governor Jim Ferguson, who said, "I never use up energy hating." He was tolerant of human vagaries. He had developed as professor and historian under the late Dr. Eugene C. Barker, for years head of the History department of the University of Texas. Barker's directness and his integrity were admirable. I myself owe considerable to him. The older he grew, the more conservative, even reactionary, he grew. He seemed in his later years to think that the masses of mankind need a sort of dictatorial direction in religion, politics, and other regions of life. While Dr. Barker became hostile, in his acrid way, to the New Deal and a strong bolster to the by-no-means-intellectual regents who deposed Rainey, mainly for being a New Dealer, Webb was strong for Franklin D. Roosevelt, as he was later for Truman. But he was never against Barker. "I did not understand him," I heard him say, "but he was my friend and supporter. He was open, generous, fearless. I remember him with respect."

Webb maintained a dim view of certain English teachers under whom he had studied in the University of

Texas. He acknowledged no debt to them in mastering the craft of writing. Some time in the 1920's he was avidly reading O. Henry and trying out his own hand on short stories. I remember one based on an electric sign above Joske's store in San Antonio that every night flashed on the picture of a cowboy roping a steer.

I wish he had written more on the craft of writing. I quote from his essay "On the Writing of Books," published in the *Alcalde,* June, 1952 (and repeated with changes and additions in his presidential address to the American Historical Association, reproduced in the Texas *Observer,* January 24, 1959):

> It takes a good deal of ego to write a book. All authors have ego; most of them try to conceal it under a cloak of assumed modesty which they put on with unbecoming immodesty. This ego makes itself manifest in the following ways: (1) The author believes he has something to say. (2) He believes it is worth saying. (3) He believes he can say it better than anyone else. If he ever stops to doubt any one of these three beliefs, he immediately loses that confidence and self-deception — that ego, if you please — so essential to authorship. In effect, the author, to write a book spins out of his own mind a cocoon, goes mentally into it, seals it up, and never comes out until the job is done. That explains why authors hide out, hole up in hotel rooms, neglect their friends, their family, and their creditors . . . they may even neglect their students. They neglect everything that may tend to destroy their grand illusion.

The longer Webb jousted with words and thoughts, the finer-tempered his blade became. His use of the specific to bring home an idea suggests in style Jesus' application of the parable. His "The American West, Perpetual Mirage" (*Harper's* magazine, May, 1957) is as brilliant as any historical essay I have read. With what economy does he set forth the core:

"The overriding influence that shapes the West is the desert. That is its one unifying force. It permeates the plains, climbs to all but the highest mountain peaks, dwells continuously in the valleys, and plunges down the Pacific slope to argue with the sea."

Webb's generalizations are conclusions drawn from and supported by the concrete:

Western history is bizarre because of the nature of what it has got. The historians and other writers do what men have always done in the desert. They make the best of what little they do have. Westerners have developed a talent for taking something small and blowing it up to giant size, as a photographer blows up a photograph.

They write of cowboys as if they were noble knights, and the cowmen kings. They do biographies of bad men, Billy the Kid, the Plummer gang, and Sam Bass, of bad women like Calamity Jane, of gunmen like Wyatt Earp and Wild Bill Hickok. . . . They blow the abandoned saloon up into an art museum, and Boot Hill into a shrine for pilgrims. In Montana Charlie Russell is better than Titian, and in the Black Hills Frederick Remington is greater than Michelangelo. Custer, who blundered to his death, taking better men with him, found a place in every saloon not already preempted to that travesty on decency and justice, Judge Roy Bean.

Some commentators have characterized Webb as a "great Texan." "We Texans," he wrote me in 1957, "have been as insular as Kansas — God save the mark." I remember well, with a certain personal shrinking, a period when his boundaries and my boundaries were to an extent circumscribed by the boundaries of Texas.

Each of us in his way passed to a perspective beyond geographical lines, though each remained deeply marked by the land he lived in and by the inhabitants of that land. The greatness of Webb was as a man. "Man thinking" — Emerson's definition of a scholar — does not have around his head a band welded there by the confines of a province, by clerical ukases, or by any other mundane restrictions. Webb was not "finely suited" to life at Oxford University. He belonged to and marked the University of Texas. It was his life. Only a few months before the end he published an opinion that it now had "within its grasp" the long sought-for status of a "university of the first class." All the while he maintained the critical judgment of "man thinking":

"Men at Oxford are free to follow their compass of truth wherever the needle points without looking over their shoulders to see what hounds are pursuing them. Professors are not even under suspicion. An Oxford man can attend a mass meeting in London and participate without jeopardizing his job. England is not afraid to have views expressed. England, with all its apparent stupidities, seems to know what a university really is."

In "For Whom the Historian Tolls," in *An Honest Preface and Other Essays,* with an introduction by Joe B. Frantz (1959), Webb provided this economical illumination:

"Articles by historians in historical journals are correct, the sentences usually — after the editors get through with them — are grammatical, and the footnotes are properly right at the bottom of the page. But one finds in them little charm, few vivid figures of speech, and practically none of that soft luminosity — an indefinable quality — which suffuses good writing.

The reader may be informed, but he is rarely lured, enthralled, or captivated by the art of the performance."

Webb's chief research was for facts to lead to understanding. His superiority as an historian lies in his perception, his power of thought, his mastery of language, his interpretations of the land and the ever evolving currents of human affairs. Not long after his first major book, *The Great Plains,* came out in 1931, Clem Yore of Colorado reported on a gathering of Western fiction writers who had been unaware of the meaning of barbed wire, windmills, the treeless plains themselves until Webb enlightened them. In his last big book, *The Great Frontier,* he interprets the Western Hemisphere as a frontier for the expansion of Europe. He says plainly and emphatically that America has been consuming irreplaceable natural resources and that prosperity based on such procedure cannot continue. He even questions the continuance of democracy. This book came out during the outrage of McCarthyism and of the House Un-American Activities Committee's blackguard betrayals of human rights. Some fanatics, without reading the book, slammed it as an "un-American" rebuke to "free enterprise."

The first Mrs. Webb, Jane Oliphant, after having been married to Walter for more than 43 years, died in the summer of 1960, survived by a daughter, Mildred, of whom father as well as mother was very fond. In December of 1961 he married Terrell Maverick, widow of the late Maury Maverick of San Antonio, vivacious in mind and body, delightful and sensible too.

Considering his love for her and considering her marrying him, he said, "This is an unexpected dividend from life." He was openly naïve in expressing joy in

her being. He had, as it were, been born again. His
happy ardency made his friends rejoice. During the summer of 1962 while he was lecturing at the University of
Alaska, she unable to accompany him as both had
planned, he airmailed a letter to her every day. He had
never seemed so eagerly active over the publication of
one of his own books as he was over publishing *Washington Wife* by Ellen Maury Slayden, the manuscript of
which Terrell Webb had foreworded. They inscribed
the book in a San Antonio bookstore the last afternoon
of Webb's life.

On the evening of March 8, 1963, two other men and
I sat down as guests with Frank Wardlaw in his home.
He said, "Walter Webb thought he would join us, but
he will be late." After conversation and "the better adjuncts of water," we went to a Mexican restaurant. Nobody knew where we were. Before we got back to our
homes a number of people had tried to telephone Wardlaw and me. About six-thirty Webb and his wife had
been found on the ground near their overturned car, he
dead and she so severely injured that she had to remain
in the hospital for three months.

Any man who has seen and been a part of life wants
to leave it before decomposing into a juiceless vegetable.
Webb died standing up, as Caesar considered it meet
for a man to die. In a flash he passed from wisdom and
happiness to the finality of death. No person who has
added as much to the heritage of human life as Walter
Webb added ceases to be. His thinking, his writing, and
his standing up will surely continue as elements of his
projected shadow.

Stanley Walker's Life Outlook

As a professional writer I have long been interested in the outlooks and the writing ways of other writers — in their sense of values more than in their techniques.

One writing man who has interested me for decades was Stanley Walker, who began his life on a ranch in Lampasas County, Texas, on October 21, 1898, and ended it on the same plot of earth with a shotgun on Sunday morning, November 25, 1962. The next day newspapers all over America chronicled his career, the apex of which was as city editor of the New York *Herald Tribune*. A tracing of that career is not in place here.

Perhaps his most widely known book is *City Editor*. He certainly won a distinct place among the writers classified geographically as Texan. I became acquainted with him in the fall of 1915 in a class of Freshman English in the University of Texas. Just ten years older than he, I was an instructor. I soon learned from his themes that he was markedly intelligent. He reported on the Austin *American* while still in the University, which he left after finishing his third year.

I don't remember seeing him again until 1931. I was in New York to take part in the promotion of a book of mine by the Literary Guild. He seemed to know everybody in the news as well as many people who were not. The book being promoted was *Coronado's Children,* tales of lost mines and buried treasures. Somebody at a dinner expressed the idea that my purpose was to turn Texas and other parts of the Southwest back to the times I was writing about. Stanley Walker ended discussion of the idea by saying, "Life changes, but changing people don't turn back." Sometimes they try. I recalled his words twenty years later while I was reading what is to me the greatest book of travels in the English language, Charles M. Doughty's *Travels in Arabia Deserta.* Interested in the life of Doughty, I learned that after writing his wonderful travel book, the language of it often as strange as the ways of Arabian nomads, he devoted himself — fruitlessly — to making modern English revert to that of Chaucer and Spenser.

Years after Stanley Walker had returned to his family's ranch in the Texas hill country and had written what may be his best book, *Home to Texas,* he wrote me about an experience from his days with the *Herald Tribune* in New York. I had written a magazine piece about that eccentric hunter of bears, who lived to himself out in the wilds, Ben Lilly. In his letter Stanley Walker said that he was summoned to the office of "an elderly, prim, tight-lipped New England spinster known as a purist on the English language and as an expert in poetry. Rather forbidding but very intelligent, she had never taken anything stronger than elderberry wine or had a date (if that's the word) and had never betrayed the slightest interest in such matters as bear-hunting, trail-driving, and sleeping on the ground. Waving your piece on Ben Lilly at me she said, 'So you know Mr. Dobie down in Texas?'

"After talking to her a while about the traditional Southwest, I told her that when we had time and could afford it, you and I would organize a pack outfit with guns, sleeping and cooking equipment, and the proper mozos, and ride with her from the headwaters of the Rio Grande in Colorado away down into the Sierra Madre of Sonora and below that even. We would take a year, I told her, if need be, sleeping on rocks and listening to coyotes recite their poetry.

" 'You're joking,' the old girl said sadly, 'but I'd rather do that than anything else in the world.' "

Stanley Walker was a newspaper, magazine, and book writer for nearly forty-five years. He had ideas; he took stands; but primarily, in books and articles as well as in newspaper pieces, he reported life as he saw it. His kind of reporting included interpretation. In reviewing a book — and he reviewed many books — he might pass judgment on it. You could bet a dollar against the hole in a doughnut that he never said it was good when he knew it wasn't.

The kind of editorial slant that some of his maturer articles took is illustrated by one he wrote for the *New York Times Magazine* on the chilling effect suffered by Texas bragging when Alaska was admitted as the forty-ninth and the biggest state of the Union. He considered that bragging had done "more harm to Texas than tick fever, the pink bollworm and Pappy O'Daniel put together." The Texas blowhard, he continued, "is like the Texas jackass, a highly durable animal. The more the average Texan studies the picture, the more he is inclined to shut up; and there is nothing in the constitution to prevent him from doing just that."

The last paragraph in the opening chapter of his last book, entitled *Texas*, which came off the press only a few weeks before he ended his writing career, reads thus: "The fight for realistic appraisal, without apologies, seems to be winning. I love Texas. I returned to the state sixteen years ago and have never regretted the move. I expect to die out in the hills and to be buried there. But I am not blind. There is much about Texas that is depressing, ugly, disgusting. Why lie about it? Why, indeed, lie about anything?"

Stanley Walker wrote on many subjects, many people, sometimes withholding an opinion, often giving it, but very seldom, if ever, suggesting action. He could have a strong opinion and at the same time keep clear of causes.

For instance, he grew a variety of peppers on his small ranch out from Lampasas, and made a variety of pepper sauces, put up in a variety of bottles, especially whiskey bottles, to give away to a variety of people. I can't imagine his raising a hand in any movement to grow pepper, to cultivate a more widespread taste for pepper sauce, or standardize the bottles for holding pepper sauce.

His mind ran to irony and sarcasm rather than to straight-out denunciation. He practiced his advice to reporters to tell a story rather than talk about it.

In 1935 he resigned his position as city editor of the New York *Herald Tribune* to become managing editor of the New York *Mirror,* a Hearst newspaper. He stayed with it only a year, an "unhappy experience," to use his words. At that time Arthur Brisbane was high in the

Hearst chain of newspapers, writing an opinionated column published in all the links of the chain. Some time after Brisbane died, Walker wrote an article on him, under the title of "They Tell Me He Was a Great Man," for the *Saturday Evening Post*. I read it and told Walker that he certainly did peel the paint off his former superior. He replied that some of Brisbane's people had written him thanking him for what he had said.

His irony was frequently well hidden from any but perceptive people. In *Texas* he writes that he had met all the governors of Texas beginning with Tom Campbell (1907–1911) and continuing into 1962. One can read through what he says on the governors and decide that he purposely avoided coming to grapples with reality. Then one comes upon a passage in which the ironic humor is plain to anybody not immersed in patriotic nonsense: "Governor Beauford Jester remarked that 'Texans are a race of people.' His successor, Allan Shivers, deserves a place in history for saying that a certain proposal was 'un-Texan.' The Jester-Shivers additions to the science of anthropology confirmed what had been suspected all along — that Texans, by golly, actually do have a genetic arrangement different from that of less favored people."

In letters to friends, Stanley Walker was apt to set down bald opinions, unsheathed in irony. In August of 1956 he wrote me: "Your dismal outlook on politics, the intelligence of the race, etc., matches mine. God Almighty, this race for Governor is the saddest of all. I'm tempted to scratch both names in the second primary and write in Jim Hogg or Byron Utrecht or Harold Higgins Young, or maybe E. M. Pease. [Byron Utrecht was political reporter on the Fort Worth *Star-Telegram;*

Harold Young is a civilized attorney at Odessa and an interesting conversationalist. E. M. Pease was governor from 1853 to 1857.] I further predict: In another 30 years only five percent of the people in Texas can read anything, even labels of catsup bottles."

It could be that Walker's prophecy on the literacy of Texans was derived from his opinion of television and its effect on the populace. "Any traveler in Texas," he wrote, "can find homes with no bathtubs and no books but with television sets — gadgets for which, in many instances, the owners go into debt. The Texan was in a difficult spot to begin with (with practically the whole rest of the world hooting at him), and now he has chosen this method to debase his mind and spirit still further. Television has been the destroyer of initiative, imagination, originality, and all the valuable inner resources. It has no doubt been a blessing to shut-ins, and has kept many dodderers off the streets and highways. Beyond that, what? I question that it has increased an awareness of the basic economic and political questions, and what it has done to the children and to grown folks who used to be able to talk with some coherence, is quite beyond measuring. Some day this monster will be turned to some human use, but its effect on Texas has been much like repeated whiffs of marijuana — in some ways worse."

Stanley Walker never had any use for jazzed-up life. He maintained a deep respect for correct language. H. W. Fowler's book *Modern English Usage* was a kind of Bible to him as a writing man. Many professors of journalism have never heard of it.

Effortlessness is often a subject for ridicule. On a recent visit Stanley Walker told this little folk tale. A man living in a house back from the road was noted for his lack of energy. One day while he was sitting in a chair on the front gallery, leaned back against a post, chewing tobacco and spitting on the floor, his wife came to the door and, looking out, said, "That's a peculiar kind of funeral procession going along there."

The man — without moving, of course — said, "I wish I could see it."

In politics Stanley Walker was a conservative. During the 1962 election he considered a prominent John Bircher stupid for supposing that he would vote to elect a John Bircher, one of the candidates, governor of Texas. Thomas Dewey and Wendell Willkie, Republican candidates for the presidency of the United States, were his friends, and he wrote a promotion book on each of them. A certain journalist's labeling him an "arch-conservative," he commented in a letter, "would class me with Alvin Owsley, H. L. Hunt, H. R. Cullen, Evetts Haley, the American Legion, Lynn Landrum — all of whom I have at one time or another denounced. True, I am something of a classicist in economics, and I try to take care of myself in the difficult world, but this thoughtless epithet surely is not right. He entirely misses the point. If I am anything I am a skeptic, a doubter, a libertarian, and I'm certainly cautious and conservative about taking up fads, quackeries and fresh suggestions for saving the world. I also admire Alexander Hamilton — Jefferson also, but Hamilton, in his diagnosis and prognosis, seems to me to have been highly accurate. I respect mankind, and have a sneaking idea that it is possible for the race to make a sort of progress, but I do not believe in the wisdom of the masses or that the Voice of the People is the Voice of God."

Two biographical facts should perhaps be added.

(1) When he came back to Texas in 1946 he brought his second wife. He gave many books to the Lampasas Public Library. In time Mrs. Walker — Ruth Walker — became the librarian and began building it up and engendering public interest in it. She is one of the choice acquisitions for Texas in sixteen years. (2) Shortly before his end Stanley Walker said, "I love life but on my own terms." A specialist had told him that he had cancer of the throat and that his larynx would have to be removed.

John A. Lomax

I SHALL not undertake to sketch the life of Lomax. It
has been pretty well done. *The Handbook of Texas,*
that remarkable two-volume compendium of life, geography, and history of Texas that Walter Prescott
Webb devised and edited, has a good sketch of John A.
Lomax. I would rather consider him as a human being
and as a landmark in preserving and popularizing the
folk songs of the United States.

When he came to Texas at the age of two with his
family from Mississippi in 1869, he settled or was settled on a farm in Bosque County about two miles from
Meridian. This farm was located on the Chisholm Trail,
or a branch of it, and here Lomax as a boy heard cowboys keep their cattle quiet at night by singing quiet
songs to them. His people, who were very poor, were not
cow people. He never was a cowboy, but before he was
twenty years old he had written down numerous cowboy songs.

In 1940, the Texas Folklore Society brought out a
volume of widely assembled personal narratives of facts
and imaginings called *Mustangs and Cow Horses.* Harry
H. Ransom, who in time became chancellor of the University of Texas, and Mody C. Boatright, who has left the

Texas Folklore Society editorship to another, were co-editors of that volume. In it there is a piece of Lomax on Peepy-Jenny, a mare that brought a colt every year on the Bosque County farm while working, and seemingly none was sold. She came to have quite a progeny of these "woods colts," as the Lomax children called them. Peepy-Jenny herself was an orphan, raised on a bottle. "A household pet," to quote Lomax, "she also became a household pest. She learned to open every gate on the place and could deftly let down any rail fence that stood in her way. Whenever in later years she or any of her family got hungry, she could open the door that led to the feed room. I used to watch her pull out the pin that held down the latch, lift the latch with her teeth, and then swiftly push open the door."

Lomax tells of driving wagonloads of wood to Meridian with Peepy-Jenny as one of the span. He always left the gate open so that all the family could accompany the wagon. They made a fine show in Meridian. His favorite horse was a son of Peepy-Jenny named Selim. "I always rode Selim to Sunday School, spelling matches and play parties," Lomax wrote. When time came for him to go off to college — and the colleges he went to were hardly in the rank of the present-day high school — he sold Selim for money to help pay for an education. As Lomax walked away from a horse trader's lot in east Dallas, Selim kept nickering to him. Lomax would almost shed tears when he remembered that parting with Selim, the son of Peepy-Jenny.

About the time *Mustangs and Cow Horses* came out, the Texas Folklore Society was publishing a few books on range men. One of them was the memoirs of a man named McCauley, whom Lomax had found and who trusted Lomax and gave Lomax his own reminiscences. I don't think any more realistic cowboy has appeared between book covers than McCauley, and certainly none more humorous. I mention this because it illustrates the early familiarity of Lomax with the type, with the people, the cow people whose songs he would recollect and make popular.

He told me the following yarn on a Bosque County rancher named Ed Nichols. This also illustrates his familiarity with ranch folk. Many years after Lomax left the Bosque County farm to get an education, he took his old neighbor Ed Nichols out to the SMS cowboy reunion at Stamford. They were sitting on the ground with another old waddie named Jeff Hanna watching the rodeo performances when Lomax noticed Will Rogers almost by his side. Will had slipped in unannounced and wanted to watch instead of being watched. However, he was glad to see Lomax and gladder still to meet the veteran cowhands Lomax introduced.

"How long you been out in this country, Jeff?" Will Rogers asked.

"Why, Will, when I come out here the sun was jest about as big as a saucer." Then Jeff went on to tell about Ed Nichols.

"Now Ed here," he said, "is one of the kindest-hearted fellers you ever see. When he was riding west from Bosque County one time he sorter found it convenient to ride in the night."

"Uh huh," and some winks.

"Well, he was coming along way late and the moon was down and it was as dark as the inside of a cow. He was in a bottom, down clost to a creek, when he begun to hear a cow bawling, but he couldn't locate her. He seemed to be near her, and he knew from the way she was going on she was in trouble and appealing for help. You know how one of them old-timey cows could talk."

"She shore could," Will Rogers agreed.

"Well, dreckly Ed here got down off his horse and begun feeling along the ground. Purty soon he came to the edge of an old well, and then he realized the cow had fell in. She didn't seem to be hurt, though, from the way she was talking. Ed knew he couldn't pull her up by hisself with a rope, but he jest couldn't ride off and leave her, on account of his soft heart.

"What you guess he did? Well, as I said, he was clost to a running creek. He went to the water and got a hat full of it and brought it back and poured it in the well. He kept packing water that way till daylight, the cow sorter floating and swimming, until finally the water was high enough for her to scramble out."

John Avery Lomax enrolled at the University of Texas in 1895 and graduated two years later. The University had been in existence only twelve years when Lomax entered it. After graduating, he remained as secretary to the president, as registrar, and as steward or manager of B Hall, the only men's dormitory ever to be located on the main campus. The combined jobs paid $75 a month.

In 1903 he went to A. & M. College to teach English at $1,200 a year. Here he gathered more cowboy songs. The A. & M. men were then predominantly rural. Long afterwards Lomax told me that he thought he'd made a mistake in giving low grades to interesting themes that were incorrectly written so far as grammar, sentence structure, spelling, and punctuation go.

In 1904 he married Bess Brown. By the time he got a scholarship in Harvard in 1906, Shirley Lomax, the first of four children, had been born. At Harvard, Lomax took a course in American literature under Professor Barrett Wendell. Barrett Wendell, to quote Lomax's *Adventures of a Ballad Hunter,* a remarkable autobiography in many ways, announced to the class that he was utterly weary of reading dissertations on Hawthorne, Emerson, Thoreau, Holmes, Poe, and other standard American writers. He said, "You fellows who have something back home, I want you to write a piece on what you know scattered over the country." When Lomax proposed writing a term theme on cowboy songs, Barrett Wendell was exhilarated. He introduced Lomax to Professor George Lyman Kittredge, perhaps the greatest scholar who has ever taught English in an American university. And Kittredge had Lomax for dinner.

The Harvard attitude toward cowboy songs was in marked contrast to the attitude Lomax had found in Texas. In his *Adventures of a Ballad Hunter* he tells of showing his roll of cowboy songs to Dr. Leslie Waggener, under whom Lomax was taking a course on Shakespeare and who also was *ad interim* president of the University of Texas. I shall quote two paragraphs.

Dr. Waggener referred me to Dr. Morgan Callaway, Jr., a Johns Hopkins Doctor of Philosophy whose scholarship is reflected in three studies, *The Absolute Participle in Anglo-Saxon, The Appositive Participle in Anglo-Saxon,* and *The Infinitive in Anglo-Saxon.* Timidly I handed Dr. Callaway my roll of dingy manuscript written out in lead pencil and tied together with a cotton string. Courteous and kindly gentleman that he was, he thanked me and promised to report the next day. Alas, the following morning Dr. Callaway told me that my samples of frontier literature were tawdry, cheap and unworthy. I had better give my attention to the great movements of writing that had come sounding down the ages. There was no possible connection, he said, between the tall tales of Texas and the tall tales of *Beowulf*. His decision, exquisitely considerate, was final — absolute. No single crumb of comfort was left for me.

I was unwilling to have anyone else see the examples of my folly. So that night in the dark, out behind Brackenridge ("B") Hall, the men's dormitory where I lodged, I made a small bonfire of every scrap of my cowboy songs. Years afterwards, an associate of Dr. Callaway in the English faculty, Dr. R. H. Griffith, asked to examine a first copy of *Cowboy Songs and Other Frontier Ballads,* published in 1910. The following morning he brought the book to my desk, thanked me for the loan, turned on his heel, and went away with no word of comment. The disfavor of my cowboy song project still survived.

After Lomax returned to Texas A. & M. College from Harvard with a master's degree in 1907, Harvard offered him a thousand dollars a year to go on with the cowboy song project, provided Texas A. & M. would give him a leave of absence from teaching. The A. & M. executives appeared to have no more interest in cowboy songs than the professors of English at the University of Texas had. They refused to grant a leave of absence. Harvard gave him three successive Sheldon Fellowships, however, and on this money, $500 a year, I believe, he went out to collect songs. His account of some individuals from whom he got songs and of circumstances under which he got them is as interesting as the narrative of any gold-rush adventurer.

When his book, *Cowboy Songs and Other Frontier Ballads,* was published, it was dedicated to Theodore

Roosevelt, "who while President was not too busy to turn aside — cheerfully and effectively — and aid workers in the field of American balladry." Also, the book reproduced a handwritten letter to Lomax from Theodore Roosevelt. And it included an introduction by Barrett Wendell. Some time after the book was published, Professor Kittredge came to Austin and Lomax took him to a Negro church, where there was a grand welcome and where Kittredge made known his great sympathy for Negro folklore of all kinds, spirituals included.

It is not correct to say, as is sometimes said, that *Cowboy Songs and Other Frontier Ballads* was the first collection of such songs to be printed. N. Howard (Jack) Thorp, of New Mexico, was a genuine cowpuncher, also a fine gentleman of generous nature with cultivation of mind that gave him perspective. In 1908 he had printed at Estancia, New Mexico, a little paperbound book of about fifty pages entitled *Songs of the Cowboys.* He carried it around in saddle pockets to sell to cowboys or anybody else with four bits to spend for it. He had some copies left a long time afterward. I saw one advertised the other day for $150. Lomax took generously from this collection without any tedious explanation.

In 1920 the Thorp book, very much extended, was brought out by that highly respectable publisher, Houghton Mifflin of Boston, Massachusetts. I saw Lomax a few days after I procured my copy and spoke of it. He had procured a copy too. I said, "I see some things in Thorp's new book that are in *Cowboy Songs.*"

"Yes," he said, "and no mention made of the source. I don't know whether to tell my publishers to bring suit or not."

He didn't, of course, and when in 1938, with the help

of his son Alan, a very much enlarged collection of *Cow-boy Songs and Other Frontier Ballads* came out, due indebtedness to Howard Thorp was acknowledged.

Lomax gave generous credit to many people. He gave generous help to many people. When I came to the University of Texas in 1914 at a salary of $1,200 a year — the salary that took Lomax to A. & M. College — Lomax was back in Austin as secretary of the Ex-Students' Association. He was publishing the first literary magazine of consequence, the only literary magazine at the time, in Texas, the *Alcalde*. It published H. Y. Benedict's *Peri-grinusings*, of great local fame. At least one sketch by John W. Thomason, who later wrote and illustrated the *Jeb Stuart* and *Lone Star Preacher* books, appeared there. Lomax offered me $100 a year to contribute a monthly feature on faculty news. Sometimes I managed to get a truth in the feature that wasn't exactly news. He would pay me twice or maybe four times a year. Anyhow, I was getting $100 for eight issues, and that was more than 8 percent of my salary. It meant more then to me than several thousand dollars might have meant later. Lomax never censored what I wrote. One day he handed me, with a smile, a letter from Bishop Kerwin of the Catholic Church, residing in Galveston, protesting what I had written on Roger Casement's "sophistry." The bishop characterized my style as that of a freshman lacking "intellectual grasp." So far as I know, he received no response to his letter.

As time went on, Lomax and I became, I won't say close friends, but very, very together friends. I doubt if I've heard any man the superior of Lomax in telling anecdotes of characters. Many of these anecdotes are in

Adventures of a Ballad Hunter. Perhaps his skill in that kind of telling reached a climax in the sketch he wrote on "Will Hogg, Texan," published in the *Atlantic Monthly* in 1940, and in 1956 published by the University of Texas Press for the Hogg Foundation. Lomax worked with Will Hogg raising money to give University of Texas students who needed help and were worth helping. I take one instance from the essay on Will Hogg:

"One Christmas morning I visited Will Hogg in a New York hotel and found him unwrapping packages. 'Here's something from home,' Will Hogg said. He unrolled six or seven silk neckties. Inside were nearly a hundred penciled signatures on a long strip of paper whose margins were splotched with smutty fingerprints. 'Christmas Greetings to Mr. Will Hogg from his friends, the newsboys of Houston, Texas.'

"Will Hogg held the ties aloft, fingered them, and then walked over toward the window and looked down on Broadway far below. He stood with his back to me for a long time. When he turned around, as if angry at his tears he blurted out, 'The damned little rascals! They ought to be horsewhipped for spending their nickels on me.' He choked again and turned back to the window."

Never forget the humanity of this man Lomax.

In 1931, Bess Brown Lomax died. In 1933, Lomax entered into a long career of collecting not only the words but the tunes of Negro and other folk songs. Alan was with him a great deal of the time. At times after he married Miss Ruby Terrill in 1934, she accompanied him on his song-hunting expeditions. He always referred to her both in writing and in speech as Miss Terrill. I don't know if he had any other name for her to her face or not, although I've been with them together various times.

I wish I could convey the sympathy and understanding Lomax had for the Negroes who sang for him into his recording machine. He and Alan took about ten thousand songs to the folksong archives in the Library of Congress. There was Iron Head. There was Lead Belly, about whom the two wrote books. There was Red Dobie, perhaps a distant relation of mine, who was expert at singing "sinful songs" as well as spirituals. To read the last half of *Adventures of a Ballad Hunter* is to enter into a character gallery of Negroes. The Lomaxes went to all the penitentiaries of the Southern states. One passage expresses John Lomax's pervading feelings toward these people: "These songs and others I heard that day I shall carry in my heart forever. And those earnest black-faced boys, dressed in grizzly gray stripes, who sang them I shall never forget. The reaction from a high pitch of emotional excitement gave me a sleepless night."

Lomax was fond of whiskey. Many a congenial time as we sat in shade of the "big elm" in our backyard, I've seen him lift his cool glass and, quoting an ancient professor of the University of Texas, say, "Here's to the sunny slopes of long ago!" and then talk on in that vein. If the slopes have not been sunny to a person, I suppose he would not want to remember them. They have been sunny for me and I love to remember them, and with them Lomax's unfailing toast.

I remember one time when he didn't drink to the sunny slopes of long ago. He and Alan had a room up the hill from our house on Waller Creek in Austin. One

evening Lomax came along about drink time. He had a
very cheerful expression on his face. I said, "Lomax,
you're just in time. We both need a drink."

He said, "No, not this evening."

I looked him straight in the eyes. I said, "You've got
to explain."

With a glad gleam in his eye, he said, "I'm on my way
to take Miss Terrill to dinner. She does not approve of
whiskey."

Several years passed, and Lomax called on me here in
Austin. He and "Miss Terrill" were back from the
Brush Country around Cotulla, where he had recorded
various vaquero songs and got my brother Elrich to sing
for him. Elrich can sing Mexican songs better than he
sings songs in English. Now Lomax wanted me to
quaver, or sing, or somehow sound what is called "The
Texas Lullaby." I can remember hearing it long, long
ago on our ranch. "Who-o-o, who-e-e, ho-ho-ho-, ha, ha,
ha," it went, no printed syllables possibly suggesting the
vocal sounds. They had a wonderfully soothing effect on
wild cattle hemmed up in the brush.

Well, the Lomaxes had a room in the Alamo Hotel
on West Sixth Street. I went down there and did the best
I could. Somebody else, I forget who, was being recorded, and Lomax seemed to get tired. I saw him go
over to the corner of the room and take a dark-looking
bottle — wasn't more than a pint — from under the bed
and, standing there facing the corner, refresh himself
with what Charles Lamb called "the better adjuncts of
water." It was his idea that Miss Terrill wasn't looking.
I was looking and I didn't know why she couldn't see.
Lomax had come back to whiskey.

While I was at Cambridge University during World

War II, Lomax in Austin got word to Bertha McKee Dobie that he wanted a certain book. She had influenza and couldn't receive him or anybody else, but he came to the house and the book was delivered by a maid. Then he stood out on the walk in front of the house and talked to Bertha Dobie as she stood at an upstairs window in something like these words: "As long as this old heart beats, I'll remember how good you've been to me and mine." In telling me this incident, she remarked, "I have done more for people who remembered it less."

During later years I sometimes felt a kind of chasm come between me and John Lomax. I don't think either ceased to respect and have a deep feeling for the other. The chasm can be illustrated by a story told numerous times by Roy Bedichek. He and Lomax had been friends, even comrades, since their B Hall days together at the University of Texas back in the 1890's. For years before his first book, *Adventures with a Texas Naturalist*, appeared in 1947, Bedi had restricted the major part of his literary production to personal letters. In 1942, Lomax wrote me: "In his letters at least Roy Bedichek has more genuine originality and downright power of expression than any other man ever connected with the University — in my opinion."

One year Bedichek was going to Denton or some other place north of Dallas on business as director of the Interscholastic League of Texas. Lomax wanted him to stay out at his home near White Rock Lake. "No," Bedichek wrote, "I'm not going to stay with you. You'll whip yourself into a frenzy and go off on a tirade against Roosevelt. I won't listen to it." Lomax replied by letter that he would not mention the name of Franklin D. Roosevelt so long as Bedichek was in his house.

Dr. W. J. Battle, who had sympathy for antagonism against Roosevelt, wanted to pay his old friend Lomax a visit. So it was arranged that Bedichek would deliver Battle and then go on and stop on his way back long enough to eat lunch and then drive to Austin. Bedichek delivered Battle and went on north. Two days later he came back. Had a fine lunch. Had a fine visit. Dr. Battle got his suitcase in the car, got himself in the car. He had already told Lomax good-bye. Bedichek told Lomax good-bye, had the car engine started. And there Lomax was standing right by him in the drive. The minute Bedichek started the car moving, Lomax began cursing, his face purple. He had kept his word, you understand, not mentioning the name of Roosevelt so long as Bedichek was his guest. Now, in rising accents it was, "God damn Roosevelt! God damn Roosevelt!" After Bedichek drove past him he could still hear the combination of God and Roosevelt.

Well, we go back to the sunny slopes of long ago. We go back to a man who more than any other made the cowboy songs and Negro songs a part of the inheritance and folklore of the world. We go back to a mighty and deep understanding of people, to a man who loved and also hated. Anybody who knew him knew where he stood.

Tom Lea

WHAT I write here cannot be otherwise than personal if I say what is in me. Tom Lea and I became friends the day his father brought us together in El Paso, in September, 1937. I left his studio with both of us hoping that he would illustrate my next book, then in the making, *Apache Gold and Yaqui Silver*. The setting for most of the tales in it is the Southwest and northern Mexico of mountains, canyons, deserts and semideserts — Tom's birthright. In time, while he was still painting the great mural in the federal courthouse in El Paso, my publisher sent him a contract. After seeing the preliminary illustrations, I wrote Tom in September, 1938:

The illimitable space, the mystery, the humanity, the stark reality of the land and the men who look for the never-to-be-found gold in that land are all expressed in your pictures — expressed with drama and fidelity. Technique is necessary, and technique has to be achieved; understanding and imagination are necessary, and they are either congenital or forever withheld. In these pictures you manifest both the achieved and the inherent. I'll probably never read the book, but I'll read your pictures over and over. They alone will make the book a joy to me as long as I live.

I feel that they are far better than what I have written. They make me feel proud and humble. Some of them make the blood come up into the back of my head and tears come into my eyes.

After fifteen years of association with them, I still look at Tom's illustrations with undiminished delight — and still have not read the book, although I have a higher opinion of the writing in it than I had at the hour of the letter. Many an illustrator would have considered the preliminary illustrations good enough for reproduction, but Tom's habit of giving his best to any work in hand was already fixed. Every picture had to be finished with printer's ink, paper, and processes in mind. It was like him to give me later, in a case, the complete set of those preliminary drawings.

Working on to perfect them, he wrote: "I need not tell you how much pleasure I am having in trying to do something for you, because in doing it for you I feel somehow that I am doing it for myself also, and both of us are doing it for our *pais*." Then a little later: "The pictures are not as good as I know they ought to be, but they are as good as I can make them at this stage of my growth as an artist." After receiving a copy of the book, he wrote: "Seeing the completed book has taught me how really little I know and how really little I have put across, as a man trying to express what he feels about this country. I just pray for future opportunities and for a long life — maybe some day I will come closer."

I used to hold that in this brief life a man should not let the future interfere with the present. Hence a fruitless dispersal of enormous portions of my time. Tom holds fast to the idea that a craftsman should not allow what he has accomplished to interfere with what he proposes to accomplish. Hence his refusal to waste himself on autograph parties and public talks. Hence his unflagging concern with better work. Yet he lives to the zenith in the Now. After he had finished a mural for Pleasant Hill, Missouri, he wrote, April, 1939: "I wish I could take satisfaction in something I've done after it is finished — but I can't. I aim high and shoot low." While working that summer on a mural design for St. Louis — a mural that would express "power and poetry" — he wrote: "At times I feel my struggle with creation somehow justified; and again, I live and work in a vicious, desperate, morbid disappointment in myself."

Late in 1939 he did nine black-and-white illustrations for a small book I wrote on John C. Duval, neither of us getting a cent out of the project, but a lot of fun. Tom has always seemed comfortable about his drawing of old Bigfoot Wallace and "Uncle John" Duval, but his next job, a mural on canvas to be placed in a new railroad station at La Crosse, Wisconsin, brought its despair. He would not defer to architects any more than he has ever deferred to an artist jury. On December 21 he wrote: "The work I have done seems to me to be a strong and sincere statement of the thrill I had when one evening last month Sarah and I stood on the top of a bluff overlooking the great Father of Waters and felt the vast mystery and poetry of the land under the gray ragged clouds of a winter storm. I have painted that scene and three men facing it. It is a simple thing and the architects dislike it. It is not a decoration but an experience." Nine days later: "I can reach no judgment concerning the work I have done until I see it in the place I painted it for — but now that I have finished, I can't take much satisfaction in it." In April, 1943, after he had been painting the war for a year and a half and had done some of his strongest work, he wrote: "I feel depressed when a job is all done and past all improvement and correction. There is always so much that escapes, forever."

Tom, nevertheless, enjoys many of his pictures. If he did not, he would not have them hanging all over his house. Two years after he had painted the most belegended wild horse of America, he wrote: "I walked in on the White Pacing Mustang here in our dining room on New Year's morning and he gave me joy. I found him still wild and free." Three years later he added: "I enjoy the picture enough to forget the inadequacy of the painter."

I have never understood how he brought himself to part with one painting, an early one. It is of two Mexicans on a cold, snowy, northern night, one with a fighting cock and one with a guitar, riding on spent beasts toward a lighted cantina far away. The yearning on their faces and in all their bodies for a warm harbor, warming drink and warmhearted companions fulfills William Hazlitt's conception of gusto in painting and my own of gusto in life. Tom traded it to an El Paso dentist for services rendered.

I knew Tom's father before I knew him. He had been mayor of El Paso and seemed designed by nature for public life. The mixture of genes peculiar to the son would have molded him, no matter the road taken, into a very different man. Constant self-discipline imposed by the will to excel in art, severe self-judgment, and strict retirement increased the differences. Yet the common sense, gusto, gaiety, generosity of soul, spontaneous congeniality, and independence of Tom Lea, Sr., are marked in the son also.

While I was roaming westward in the thirties, I frequently got to El Paso and saw Don Tomás, as Mexicans there called their lawyer and patron. He spent a substantial part of his income from a good practice grubstaking prospectors and investing in wildcat mines that never paid off. In riches of undying hope he was one of Coronado's true children. Born in Missouri in 1877, he had soldiered in the Spanish-American War and studied law in the Kansas City Law School, reporting at the same time for the Kansas City *Star,* before he headed southwest. That was in 1901. He was soon at home in Mexico. On one pack trip he rode from Parral across the Sierra Madre to Colima against the Pacific. As much at ease with the Spanish language as with himself, he would, after he became established in law, sometimes stand up in court and correct the official interpreter. When the Mexican Revolution broke out in 1910, he was ready for the exiles from across the Rio Grande. Ex-President Victoriano Huerta was one of his clients.

His first job after settling in El Paso was as a bill collector on horseback. One morning while standing in a lumberyard with his employer, he saw a girl dressed in a red coat with brass buttons walking toward the high school. "The liquefaction of her clothes" or something else made him bold to ask the boss who she was and how he could meet her. "Her name is Zola Mae Utt," the boss answered. "She goes to the Baptist Sunday School." The Baptist Sunday School had a recruit the following Sunday. They were quickly engaged. She taught piano lessons for four years while he waited for clients and roamed the country. His first case was defending a Negro for killing a Mexican; his fee was $9. Tom and Zola Mae were married in 1906. He was police judge when their firstborn let out his first squall in the early morning of July 11 the next year. The judge-father celebrated the event by freeing every man who had been jailed for drunkenness or vagrancy.

He had as law partner Robert Ewing Thomason, for seventeen years Congressman from the El Paso district and now United States District Judge. They were consulting over a third partner. "I practice law with the city directory," Tom, Sr., said.

"I practice it with Moffat's form book," Thomason said.

"Let's bring in Gideon McGrady," Tom, Sr., exploded. "He knows law." There was plenty of criminal practice that required little law. After picking his jury, the question with Tom, Sr., was whether he should give it the "round treatment" or the "flat treatment" — tears or no tears.

His impulses were quick and strong and he often obeyed them with fervid alacrity. On Thanksgiving Day of 1940, I happened to be in El Paso. The writing of *The Longhorns* was behind me and young Tom was illustrating it. I had said that I was going to write a book about Don Coyote. Tom Lea, Sr., organized a party that began in his home and ended across the Rio Grande. At his home he presented me, out of his very fine collection, with a unique Casas Grandes pot with a coyote head in bas-relief on one side and a badger head on the other. At the restaurant in Juárez, where he made life burgeon, he had us all sign a document that he had drawn up honoring *"el Jefe de los Coyoteros"* and pledging the Coyoteros "to laugh and be happy and do the best we can." He kept the pledge until a day in 1945.

The Lea home was a happy one, especially at mealtime. "My mother always kept herself and everything else under control," Tom says. "Church did not mean narrowness to her but a living goodness." After she died in 1936, Tom painted, as a memorial to her, a mural representing the baptism of Christ by John the Baptist. His father joined him in presenting it to her church. In December, 1952, after having gone for twenty-eight years without listening to a sermon, Tom was confirmed with his wife Sarah in the Episcopal Church. He had found what he had been looking for.

His parents always wanted him to be what he wanted to be. At the age of three, his mother guiding his hand, he wrote a letter to his father, absent in Kansas City. "Dear Dad, hurry home," and with unguided hand drew on the sheet of paper a picture of a man with buttons on coat and hat on head. Somewhat later a local teacher doubted that he could make a living by art. Relatively few artists do make a living that way. This teacher, Miss Gertrude Evans, now of San Diego, California, preserved a poem that Tom wrote when he was sixteen:

I am the wind on the top of the mountain.
Through ages I have whispered to the sympathetic grass,
And whistled little tunes to the stiff-faced rocks
Who seem never to hear.

At seventeen Tom was graduated from high school. Summers horseback on ranches out from El Paso and hunts in the mountains gave him something he would use later. He does not hunt now. His general schooling has been mainly from "the life-blood of master spirits." Reading great books whets but never slakes the thirst for greatness. Tom's grasp of any book he has read is as definite as his knowledge of Spanish armor, a suit of which he procured from Hollywood and put on a man out in the desert in order to portray a Spanish conquistador correctly. He singles out as special enrichers of his life Maud Durlin Sullivan, librarian of the El Paso Public Library, and the master printer of the Southwest to whom she introduced him. "She showed me what a fine book is; Carl Hertzog showed me how one must be made. Their arts, their understanding, have improved my own."

Collaboration between Tom Lea and Carl Hertzog came years ago to seem as natural as swimming naked in summertime in a deep pool of clear, cold water. It is based on the joy of producing something beautiful. That basis goes also for the history of the King Ranch that Tom is now writing and illustrating on contract and that Carl is to print. I have had at least three bully times with them myself, notably in bringing out a new edition of Charlie Siringo's *A Texas Cowboy*, first published in 1885, which Tom illustrated, Carl designed, and I wrote an introduction for. Royalties from a generous publisher did not diminish our fun on this project.

But back to schooling. In 1924, financed by his father, Tom went to the Art Institute of Chicago. There John Norton, his *maestro*, burned this truth into his consciousness: "The worst crime an artist can commit is to kid himself." Norton, a noble nature, was primarily a muralist, and Tom intended to be. Like marble — and also like brandy, according to one of Dr. Johnson's flashes — the mural makes heroes. No matter what subject may be painted into a mural, a Tom Benton Missouri mule or a Tom Lea pioneer woman of muscular back and bottom holding a dented water bucket, this medium is for high-reaching imagination; it belongs by rights to the "lust for the illimitable" and to a brush of comet's tail. Some of Tom's strongest and noblest painting is on walls; certain of his drawings and canvases seem to reach toward the heroic spaciousness and perspective of a vast hall. "Trail Herd," called also "Lead Steer," illustrates what I mean. But from the beginning of his career Tom seems to have accepted the limits imposed by art in every form. He early learned what Abraham Lincoln advised a mother to teach her child: to deny himself. He contains himself; he is the antipodes of diarrhetic Thomas Wolfe.

After two years in the Art Institute, Tom became sole paddler of his own canoe. Whenever John Norton had commissions for murals, he hired Tom as an assistant in his studio. For nearly fifteen years Tom supplemented his income by hackwork, laying out advertising, designing menus, et cetera. "Making money with his craft may give an artist a certain discipline," he says, "but he pays for it in precious time, and I believe that no real artist has any of that to spare." In 1930 he made enough money on a quick job of decorating a Chicago nightclub to go to Europe. He spent four intense months studying Italian frescoists of the Renaissance.

Back in Chicago, he hungered more and more for the Southwest. The mighty prose of Charles M. Doughty's *Travels in Arabia Deserta,* which he was reading at this time, illuminated for him by similarities the starkness, the spirit and life — especially Spanish life — of his own land. In 1933 he "got enough ahead to get out of Chicago for good." He went to Santa Fe and built a one-room adobe house nine miles out of town and "tried to paint." Hard times of the depression were on, but work as part-time staff artist at the Laboratory of Anthropology helped out income from scarce odd jobs and gave an apprehension of Indian designs that has not, it seems to me, been without influence on the naked simplicity of Tom's own designs.

In 1936, Nancy Lea, Tom's first wife, died and he moved back to El Paso — under Mount Franklin. He was through with art colonies forever. Nancy Lea, as demonstrated by the posthumous publication of her *Notebook* — in an edition of only twenty-five copies — was a woman of sinewed and active intellect. The last entry in the *Notebook* contains a pertinence:

"Tom is so terribly wrong in his belief that one can get at the heart of any matter by wallowing in it. He shall never see his Southwest until he climbs to the top of a very tall tree and looks down and sees that his Southwest is so infinitesimal it cannot be picked out. Then, God willing, he will see the whole of things, the one unity of life."

A very tall tree was on ahead. In the spring of 1941, Tom began painting World War II for *Life* magazine. He was aboard a destroyer in the Atlantic when Pearl Harbor came, and then for four years worked full time as war artist–correspondent. He traveled more than 100,000 miles, saw life from many new perspectives, looked upon death in the terriblest forms, and brooded in the land of Confucius.

He was on the aircraft carrier *Hornet* not long before it went down. Back in El Paso to paint what he had seen and sketched on the *Hornet,* he wrote, November 22, 1942:

It seems to me now when I lie sleepless and see again the brilliant sea and sky, and feel the hot iron decks, and smell the burning oil, and hear the roar of the planes and flames and the rumble and crack of the guns, that I carry with me the burden of having to tell my countrymen who have not been there what it is like to fight and die in iron ships and hurtling planes on far oceans. Out there men have to build strong altars in their hearts. Now I feel small and incapable, unworthy of a joy in homecoming that I never earned. It would be intolerable if I did not hope that I come back to be a kind of witness for all my comrades on the distant seas, those high in the blazing sky, and those down in the lightless waters forever. It is a terrible burden to have to paint pictures to be worthy of those strong altars.

For nearly six months he painted furiously. In March, 1943, he wrote urging me to accept an invitation to lecture for a year on American history at Cambridge University. "You might come back to tell us even more about Texas, after you had looked at it for a while from the other side of an ocean . . . I'm sure I've seen new colors and more beloved forms in Mount Franklin since I got home from the Solomons."

By the middle of May he had finished the "long grinding effort" on eighteen *Hornet* pictures and delivered them in New York. They and thirty-six other Tom Leas went into a collection of fewer than two hundred war pictures exhibited by *Life* in the National Art Gallery in Washington, the Metropolitan in New York, and other museums over the nation.

"Strangely," Tom wrote of his latest work, "I never slowed down, never lagged in spirit. Each morning I felt renewed, and able. I groaned and swore and said I was tired, but by golly I know the last pictures were stronger and better than the first. I believe that when you have something vital to say, nothing can take that vitality from your effort." On another occasion he said, "If you want to do a thing enough, you find a way to do it, now. My firm conviction is that what a man wants to do must be done NOW — not five years hence."

Now, but never slapdash, never glibness to cover up ignorance, never fuzzy impressions in place of clarity, always a consciousness of form that has become as instinctive in the artist as the pushing down of a tree's roots toward moisture or the pushing up of a seed's sprout toward light. In 1945, after the war was over, Carl Hertzog printed in an edition of 500 copies Tom's *Peleliu Landing* — a folio, very scarce now, of fewer than 11,000 words, with ten drawings that burn into the soul. No war correspondent that I have read has surpassed this as a record of reality. The prefatory explanation of the book reveals the *vitality* and the *now* in Tom's nature and also in his manner of work:

This is not a page from a history book, not an account of a battle. It is the simple narrative of an experience in battle; like combat itself, such a narrative is bound to be personal, confused, benumbed, and in its deepest sense lonely. D-morning, 15 September 1944, I landed on Peleliu Island, about fifteen minutes after the first troops hit the beach, with marines under command of Captain Frank Farrell. I remained under fire for the first thirty-two hours of the assault. As a *Life* War Artist my purpose in going ashore was to record the United States Marines in combat. On the beach I found it impossible to do any sketching or writing; my work there consisted of trying to keep from getting killed and trying to memorize what I saw and felt under fire. On the evening of D-plus-one I returned to a naval vessel offshore where I could record in my sketch book the burden of this memory. Before my hand steadied I put down the words and pictures that compose this book. The narrative is printed here as I first wrote it except for minor chronological rearrangement. The sketches are untouched.

Tom was maturing. Six weeks after Peleliu he wrote me from home back in El Paso:

I came as close to being killed as a man can possibly be, during the first two hours on the beach. I see no good reason why I am proud of being such a damn fool as to walk into that thing voluntarily. But reason or not, I am proud. I can now make a report on the war which is War itself, the final war of the man with the dirt of the earth in his face, the war of the man who carries a gun and a knife, who kills with his hands and spills blood and guts on the ground.

I am not going to "interpret" that war with my painting. I am trying simply to paint precisely and exactly and absolutely truly what I saw with my own two eyes. Nothing else. These are to be literal pictures, to be taken literally. Few painters have ever seen such things, and certainly none I know of has painted them. . . .

I find that as my painting goes deeper it gets harder to live with and I suffer agonies trying to bring to it those things that grow as the understanding grows. It is strange to believe that I am becoming a better painter while the pains of creation increase instead of diminish. The thing that I am after is so very far up the lonesome road afoot.

In my more optimistic moments I think about trying to write. Someday I am going to. But now is a time to take in everything I can, to see, to hear, to feel. The time to write about them is when they assume a larger design than I can see now, assume meanings I cannot yet fathom and relate. I will quit painting any day to sit with you by that little fire in the mountains. Goat ribs and frijoles will be just right.

Unlike many other artists and writers, Tom was not swept out of his orbit by the war and by the stupidities and meannesses of men in years that followed. He has never joined the protesters against evil men spreading evil ignorance and prejudice. "I am likely to judge a man according to how decent or indecent he is to human beings," he said to me once. He looked into the features of Chiang Kai-shek and sized him up as a "thug" and painted him as such. *Life* did not reproduce the portrait. Tom would starve rather than lie in paint or words for any amount of money. "I am angry and radical about only two things really," he wrote late in 1945, "thickness in the human skull, hardness in the human heart. I look the black world in the face, but cannot feel despair." Then a year later: "My studio seems a quiet, solid place in this yammering, unsolid world. About the only place I stand with any confidence is in front of my easel. There I feel happiness. I'm deeply grateful to be able to work every day at something I think is worth doing — and in working be so tired at night that I can sleep." This was while he was doing the series of pictures on Western beef cattle now owned by the Dallas Museum of Fine Arts. And in Mexico he had come closer to fighting-bulls.

Without long and absorbed lookings-out from "a very tall tree" in the Pacific, Tom could not have written *The Brave Bulls.* Right after he had finished the manuscript he brought a carbon to the Cypress Mill Ranch where Holland McCombs (of *Time-Life-Fortune*) and his wife Marjorie used to gather a few friends for a two- or three-day session over the Fourth of July. While some of us were immersed in the chapters, our talk turned on literary treatment of death and of the word *death* in titles. Green Peyton observed that all the good titles containing the word had been used up. I began quoting Sir Walter Raleigh's sublime apostrophe at the conclusion of his *History of the World:* "O eloquent, just, and mighty Death! whom none could advise, thou hast persuaded; what none hath dared, thou hast done. . . ."

Tom literally leaped from his chair. Eyes flashing and voice enriched by emotion, he cried out, "AND MIGHTY DEATH — that is the title for my novel. That *is* the novel."

As soon as we got back to Austin from Cypress Mill Ranch, we read some pages from great Raleigh and went to De Quincey's "Oh! just, subtle and mighty opium!" — the most successful sentence modeled upon another that I know of in English literature. Tom had once thought of *The Shadow of the Horn* as a title. In the end it remained *The Brave Bulls.*

About two months before this 1948 gathering at Cypress Mill, A. Phimister Proctor's statue "The Seven Mustangs" had been unveiled in front of the Texas Memorial Museum in Austin. Tom and Sarah came to our home on the way to the ranch. I drove them to the bronze mustangs and left them to run an errand. When I came back, perhaps fifteen minutes later, tears filled Tom's eyes and his voice was choked — not only for the beautiful bronze but for the inscription chiseled into the granite pedestal. "Frank, it's so beautiful," he cried.

Before he got into the illustrations for *The Longhorns,* we made a trip together through the Brush Country, up into Oklahoma and out on the Staked Plains. We saw relics of the longhorn breed, crossed trails that herds of them once beat out, slept on grass where they once grazed. When we met a cowman who belonged to the breed, Tom had to draw his features. When we saw a wild steer plunging in a chute, he went half-wild himself putting down on pad and in his brain the eyes, muscles, and spirit of the animal. We went to the Rancho Randado, far down toward the lower tip of Texas, stuffed with lore about it from my rancher friend Tom East. It was one of the earliest ranches in that region and became famous for its Spanish horses. While we lingered at an earthen tank to which vaqueros used to race Randado *manadas* and in which mustangs of Randado blood once quiveringly drank under protection of darkness, I noticed that Tom seemed to be possessed by something — some idea, some vision, some recollection — I knew not what. Many times have I wished that I had not suggested leaving so soon. Shortly after returning to El Paso, he wrote: "I have been working very hard [on the illustrations] with a fine shining happiness and health in my heart." Months later he sent me Number One of a hundred numbered and signed copies of *Randado* — an illustrated poem, in apostrophic prose as well as verse, of "proud free men and wild horses."

After the success, both financial and literary, of Tom's first novel, some people predicted that he would quit painting for writing. The univalve does not readily comprehend the bivalve. Because a man learns to ride, he need not stop walking. Many a painter lesser than Michelangelo has also written, sculptured, and architectured. A bronze of Tom Lea's composition would not surprise me. He has lately spent much time on designs for a new public library in El Paso, and is going to paint — free — the mural for its Southwestern Room. He expects, much to my joy, to keep on painting.

He writes standing up to a typewriter on a desk

mounted on blocks in his ample studio. "I sort of like this writing business," he says. *Like* is a weak word. In the midst of *The Brave Bulls* he communicated to his publisher-editor, Angus Cameron: "I wake it, sleep it, eat it, drink it, and dream it." Toward the end of *The Wonderful Country* he wrote me: "Writing a book is like setting out on a long, long journey. The road gets rough and night sets in and you think of the pleasures of home. But by God you have seen some things on the trip."

For twenty-two years art alone made a living for Tom and his household. Novels have added to daily bread and given him the assurance of time in which to work. No painting project carried out by him has demanded the *prolongation* of toil put into each of his novels. If he ever paints, in all the amplitude and detail he once planned, the "Microcosmography of the Southwest," that business will wear the soles off his feet and the soul out of his body.

The style of his writing is that of his art. Always he is the scientific craftsman. Economy, precision, logic in relationship between all parts and the whole are inherent in every drawing, every painting, every page of his making. No surplus word, line, shadow, suggestion of emotion or assertion of fact pads any particle. He files to the bone. He spent three days drawing the longhorn head design for the University of Texas Press. He made half a dozen drawings of a dismounted cowboy to get a foot and the weight on it right. Any person who scrutinizes the pants legs on one of his men will realize bones and muscles under the cloth. He wrote 40,000 words before he got the first chapter, of less than 2,500 words, in *The Brave Bulls* to suit, knowing before he wrote a word, however, what he wanted. After writing pages on the coming of spring, for *The Wonderful Country,* he sublimated them into: "A mockingbird sang from a budded cottonwood." In the throes of writing, his practice is to fill heavy paper ice sacks with discarded sheets and then to burn the accumulation. "There will be no variorum edition of Tom Lea."

Multum in parvo involves not only rigorous exercise of the "art of omission" but also discovering the salient, often at the cost of long search, and then the art of revealing it. A few details in some of Tom's small drawings say so much that the character sketches of Chaucer's Prologue — the greatest portrait gallery ever written — come to my mind. The sand-cut, windswept, sun-jerked head of a cavalryman prefacing Chapter III in *The Wonderful Country* and the climax of carnal desire in a woman's mouth accomplished by three lines, at the head of Chapter V in *The Brave Bulls,* are examples.

Nor will he pick his fruit before it is ripe. His well seep-flows rather than gushes, though it seems to me freer in his art than in his fiction. Anyhow, he understands mulling. He likes "to wait until the ideas get so strong I can't stand it any longer not to put them down. Then they'll come out whole."

Tom's comments on two masters are a revelation of his own nature and manner. After procuring the Putnam translation of *Don Quixote,* he wrote:

I went three-fourths of the way through Volume I and then — I hate to confess it — bogged down, just as I have always bogged. The vast, diffused leisure of the tale's telling somehow finally kills my interest in it. In that tome I find a page of sheer grandeur followed by chapters of sheer verbiage. I contrast it often in my mind with Voltaire's *Can-*

dide — which I re-read every year or so, always with delight and wonder. There are no pages of grandeur comparable to the immense brooding tragic irony of the pathetic Knight — but every sentence of *Candide* speaks mordantly of the matter in hand, carrying the reader without a pause for breath along the rough road of the world. I read the sad tale of Candide as a high, true example of how to write and what to write about.

An upright panel on a wall in Tom's studio contains three geometric forms, each enclosing Chinese characters. The form at the base is square — Finite Earth; a triangle above it represents Aspiring Mankind; the apex of the triangle points to a circle — Infinite Sky.

Tom Lea, based on Finite Earth, brightens any person he likes with the eagerness for life that flows from him. When I am with him I enjoy his company so much that after we have talked half the night I am too much stimulated to sleep the other half. Maybe sometimes we settle some *hoti's* business, discover the rim of some little planet new to ourselves, but recollection of the talk gives me the impression of freshened life, pictures of the human comedy, and laughter. Tom can laugh until he cries. There is generally more humor in his talk and in his drawings than in his writing. Also, he is a wonderful listener. In writers and artists of small caliber, the striving to create often absorbs eagerness for life apart from work; in Tom, each stimulates the other — but perhaps to any devoted and unceasing craftsman of talent, everything positively experienced calls out for translation through his medium. Artist and man come to be inextricably blended. Noble art cannot come out of an ignoble man, but unless a noble nature stands on guard, ignoble art sometimes escapes him.

When he learned that our dear and delightful old friend, Charles P. Everitt of New York, dealer in and knower of rare books, a geyser in reminiscent talk, as avid for comradery as Sir Toby Belch — and with a share of Sir Toby's thirst — was ill, Tom made a drawing of him and sent it for his last Christmas. "He was a wonderful man who made me feel that being alive was an adventure, exciting, funny, tragic, ironic, and completely worth living."

That fighting bull of fire and black death, that longhorn steer overlooking in majesty the grasses of a continent, that white stallion pacing free of his pursuers with the foreverness of "forever wilt thou love and she be fair," that rider to his own destiny over the shining plain, that other rider whom the hills of Mexico will envelop but cannot obliterate, that lone town of life unseen, all express a vitality that Tom once described in himself: "When I get up in Mexico City and walk out upon the street, I feel as if something excitingly fine were just about to happen."

A Magazine and Its Editors

WHEN the first issue of the *Texas Review*, subsidized by the University of Texas, appeared in June, 1915, I was on the campus as a first-year grader of freshman themes. Stark Young, the editor, I knew only slightly — and timidly. Technically, he did not belong to the English department; he was professor of comparative literature and was regarded by the wardens of pure scholarship in the English department as a poacher and debaucher of standards. For them the standard resided in the Teutonic Ph.D. system, based on Anglo-Saxon and bent on solidifying the spirit of literature into studies of grammar and form. Stark Young stood for belles lettres, and in his writing inclined toward the belletristic. He was in no way a revolutionist, but the stand of the conservatives forced him into the position of one. Most of the downs and some of the ups in the English department were for him. The members of his staff were all University of Texas professors, but the contents of the magazine showed that he did not expect it to be professorial in either tone or matter.

The christening article was by one of Stark Young's several literary friends on the other side of the Atlantic — Edmund Gosse, critic, poet, essayist, in war-wrapped

England. The editor himself wrote: "The *Texas Review* comes into the world with no mission. . . . It has in mind the law of thought and life and letters only." Strong advice had been given him, he said, "to let your magazine reek of the soil." But

. . . I ask Texas cowboys to reek and I get a silly cowboy song, an imitation of Longfellow's worst or of After the Ball. . . . The East of Texas is like Mississippi and Ohio and Middle France; the South is like Louisiana and Trieste; Austin is violet and open like Greece; and the West reminds me always of Mexico and North Africa. What then? We shall presently reek of the whole world — ah, that we only could, for that is what true literature has done forever . . .

The *Review* was to continue a good while before writers for it gave evidence that seepage of human life into the ground on which they stood had passed into them.

The most brilliant — and the most prophetic — piece in the new magazine was an essay on "Wealth and Its Ways," by Lindley M. Keasbey, another thorn in the side of academic conservatism at the University of Texas. Walter Prescott Webb says that he was the only professor who ever made him think. Since he would not fit into history, economics, or any other department, that of "Institutional History" had been designed for him. The first paragraph of his essay is sufficient to illustrate the cast of his mind and to suggest how welcome he would be to a present-day board of regents ignorant of the place of skepticism and intellectual freedom in the utopia of conformity and money-making.

Wealth is a word of several significations, for the first of which see St. Paul's Epistle to the Corinthians: "Let no man seek his own, but every other man's wealth," an injunction followed to the last figure by financial brethren highest in the faith. Wheretofore, lest those accustomed only to capitalistic concepts should mistake St. Paul's intent, revisionists, with scholarly naïveté, have altered the original rendering to read: "Let no man seek his own, but every other man's good." The Church of England is more conservative. Her communicants cut down the civil list, to be sure; for their king, however, they still pray: "Grant him in health and wealth long to live." And we, with our plutocrats and proletarians, our billionaires and beggars, call our country the American commonwealth!

The anti-German fervor accompanying America's entry into World War I drove Keasbey from Texas. Stark Young remained only long enough to edit two numbers of the *Review;* then he left for Amherst College and thence for the position of dramatic critic on the *New Republic.* Under the editorship of Dr. Robert A. Law, professor of English at the University of Texas, the *Review* entered the second phase of its existence.

I myself had little correspondence with the *Texas Review* entered the second phase of its existence.
the army for two years, for another year managed a ranch, and was in Oklahoma when its change of life came. The two essays of mine that it published I have just reread with humiliation. The first, "On the Seasonableness of Reading," overuses damnably the "accursed adjective" and the cussed adverb; it has a valid idea but strains. The second, "The Cowboy and His Songs," is sentimental, unrealistic, dishonest. I am ashamed of having written it.

I suppose I was a continuous subscriber to the *Texas Review.* I recall that when we moved to Oklahoma in the fall of 1923, I burned my file, along with much other paper considered not worth moving. Some years later I got all the back numbers. Various contributions in the magazine that I had no desire to read at the time they appeared now interest me. One such is on the mob spirit, by J. E. Pearce, who was a bold puncturer of windbags and social superstitions. The *Review* has always published poetry, or verse. I doubt if it has published any better than Leonard Doughty's translations of Heine:

> *In the north a lonely pine tree*
> *Stands on a hill of snow,*
> *And over his white-swathed slumber*
> *The frozen north winds go.*

> *He dreams of a slender palm tree*
> *In a far fair Eastern land,*
> *Longing toward his longing,*
> *From the burning sun and sand.*

Doughty was a solitary original, streaked by genius, who never found his place in the world of barbaric yawps. His contribution came through John A. Lomax, who edited the *Alcalde,* the magazine for alumni of the University of Texas, which he made at times more interesting than the *Texas Review.* Doughty's friends were Lomax and Roy Bedichek. Bedichek was editing the *Interscholastic Leaguer,* into which he sometimes injected wise thoughts.

Dr. Law doggedly kept the magazine going through the difficult years of World War I and on; he built a solid foundation, but could not magnetize writers of vitality. The contents of his magazine were often typified by "studies" fitted for interment in the *Publications of the Modern Language Association:* "Some Aspects of Plato's Style," "Some Contemporary Criticism of Dr.

Johnson," "Some Aspects of the Modern Novel," "The Sonnet in Texas Literature," "Cressid and Chaucer," "The Intellectual Inheritance of Thoreau," "Emerson and Swedenborg," "The Influence of Carlyle on Tennyson," "Modern Psychology and the Problem of Vocational Guidance." Such could not quicken either the quick or the dead.

The University of Texas administrators paying the printing bills were much relieved in 1924 to turn the magazine over to Southern Methodist University men who had a tenuous backing from their administrators. Change of name to *Southwest Review* did not suggest by any means all the changes in editorial policy to come.

The new editor of the new review, Jay B. Hubbell, announced in the first issue, October, 1924, that the magazine "will be national in its outlook, but will especially encourage those who write on Western themes, for it is a magazine for the Southwest." In a letter to me he wrote that "critical articles on literary subjects are easy to get, but good articles on politics, social affairs and Southwestern topics in general are hard to get. Good verse seems harder to get than good prose." He could have added that mediocre verse is always more plentiful than good stationery. The first issue, representative of issues to follow, contained an essay on "Western Interpreters" by Andy Adams, a devastating analysis of Jim Ferguson by Charles W. Ferguson, John William Rogers's one-act play *Judge Lynch,* and other reflections of the Southwest, as well as contributions from Gamaliel Bradford and Barrett H. Clark that would have been in place in the *Atlantic, Scribner's,* or *Century* — and had probably been rejected by the editors of those magazines.

No single item in the new *Review* would have been

exactly foreign to the old one, though the contrary was not true. It had a new emphasis, a new perspective, a new vitality. John McGinnis, one of the advisory editors, had been editing the book page of the Dallas *News,* and was making it the best in several states — as it continues to be under the editorship of younger men associated with him in their youth. I had just brought out *Legends of Texas* through the Texas Folklore Society and would soon be back at the University of Texas — from what seemed like exile in Oklahoma — giving a course in Life and Literature of the Southwest. I was about to write books, and McGinnis was about to influence me to turn them over for publication to the going-to-be Southwest Press in Dallas. As editor, salesman, and general promoter of the Texas Folklore Society publications, I was aware of the power required of a publisher for national distribution; as editor of a book page, McGinnis was familiar with the operation of both the best and the worst publishers. Neither of us was realistic. We dreamed of a press in Texas that would be independent of New York and would nurture writers and culture belonging to the Southwest. I guess we were "taking our stand" for the Republic of Texas. The university presses of Oklahoma, New Mexico, and Texas were farther off than any eye could see.

Something brisk was stirring in the air over the Southwest. "Art was upon the town," as Whistler said of another time and place. Including artists as interpreters of the Southwest enlivened and enriched the *Review.* Walter Webb was forging toward interpretations of the Land of Little Rain that were to make a landmark in American History outlooming Turner's thesis on the frontier. Stanley Vestal- was a promise in Oklahoma.

Mary Austin, Frank Applegate, Witter Bynner, and other matured writers in New Mexico became strong supporters of the quarterly burgeoning in Dallas. Mc-Ginnis knew where to go for new blood, and he went. But if any writer figured that a contribution to the *Review* would buy unconsidered praise of his next book on the Dallas *News* book page, he did not know the gay and prideful incorruptibility of the editor.

On fire with eagerness to see the development of a culture from native materials and to have natives recognize significances in the natural things all around us, to hold the mesquite on the Nueces as dear as Wordsworth held the "four fraternal" yew trees of Borrowdale, I came to regard the *Southwest Review* as the voice of salvation. The recognized fact that comparatively few people listened to the voice was no more of a damper to me than it was to the devoted souls putting out the magazine. In June, 1925, Hubbell wrote that subscriptions, at $2 a year, had grown from the fifteen inherited from the *Texas Review* to 430 — also, that Southern Methodist University could not afford further subsidy and that money had to be raised somehow.

A few enlightened citizens in Dallas began underwriting the *Review* with more or less regular donations, and eventually the University authorities stabilized the *Review* budget (including, the past dozen years or so, provision for regular payment to writers, besides ample funds to meet printing bills). I have never had anything to do with raising money for the magazine, a killing undertaking for editors, but in making lectures over Texas I used to tell my audiences that anybody who was civilized and had two dollars should subscribe and that I would take the money. I doubt if more than a dozen people responded directly over that many years of such soliciting. Soon after *Coronado's Children* came out, in 1931, I donated to the *Review* my part of the admission fees to a telling of tales in the Southern Methodist University auditorium, and thus helped raise money to print one issue.

In 1927 Hubbell left for Duke University and became increasingly active in projects more academic than the *Review*. George Bond had been the editor a year before Hubbell left. Sometimes I hardly knew who was the official editor. Those were buoyant days. Whenever I got to Dallas, which was several times a year, Johnny Mac (McGinnis) would get Henry Smith and me, sometimes with Lon Tinkle, John Chapman, or Herbert Gambrell, into a fish house and there we would make medicine over life, literature, and the *Southwest Review*. Occasionally Mac irritated me by not answering a letter, though he wrote many letters, despite his philosophy on correspondence. This philosophy he attributed to Dr. R. S. Hyer, whom I knew as president of Southwestern University and who was the nearest approach to greatness I have known among college and university presidents. His maxim was, according to McGinnis, "Why write? Eventually you'll see the man!"

Mac riled some contributors by not acknowledging, rejecting, or accepting unsolicited manuscripts. Occasionally an author who had given up hope of ever hearing from the editor would receive copies of an issue of the magazine containing his piece, perhaps drastically revised. More than one author of a manuscript that I had suggested sending in appealed to me. If McGinnis did not want to hurt a writer's feelings by telling him what he thought of an unpublishable something, he was

likely to put it away in a drawer, where queries concerning it piled up until some assistant returned it with
a horror-struck note of apology.

Not answering letters never weighed on Mac's con-
science, I judge. He was a night owl and would talk
until the cows came home and bawled to be milked, and
his talk and the stimulation he gave you to talk prolonged tarrying. He liked to recall to me that I was the
first contributor to his book page outside the Dallas
News staff; I wrote many reviews for him, getting books
I wanted free, and also a little money. It was then, and
is now, an advantage for the *Review* to be edited by an
individual in contact with all sorts of current writers.
Mac egged me on to write more for the *Review* by telling me that in decades to come thesis writers would be
combing its files to examine my contributions. This did
not stir me so much as his assuring me over and over
that he and Henry Smith recognized in my prose the
rhythms that I used to strive for as much as I now increasingly strive for precision and economy and against
the stubborn averseness of disparate particles of thought
and of words and facts to flowing as harmoniously together in composition as trees and bushes and rocks and
grass flow down the side of a mountain. Everything good
writing requires seems to come only through unremit-
ting strife — and I like it.

The devotion of a "passionate few" editors is what
has kept the *Review* in a constant state of both being
and becoming. The coalescing force for many years was
John McGinnis, but the drudgery and much responsibility were on younger men sharing his eagerness for a
superb magazine. Along in the thirties the magazine

would certainly have died had Henry Nash Smith not given up everything else but his teaching to keep it going. In his quiet way he wrote me: "It has been a tenet of mine that an over-meticulous sense of duty is a detriment to anyone who intends to write." Henry can write and he intended to write, but at this time he was exemplifying a fact about the best of editors — creative editors. They usually write little, not from want of power, but because they spend their powers on the writings of others and on the machinery of getting them into printed form.

A quarter of a century before awarders of the Nobel and Pulitzer prizes crowned William Faulkner, Henry Smith wrote one of the most penetrating criticisms of his work yet written by anybody. Thereby hangs a chapter of *Southwest Review* history. In 1931 Henry flew to Oxford, Mississippi, to interview Faulkner and get something from him for the *Review*. Editors with big money were not at that time running over each other for the Faulkner output. Henry brought back some vivid impressions and a story of about 5,000 words entitled "Miss Zilphia Gant." John McGinnis may possibly have considered it inappropriate for the *Review* to publish at that particular time — not for the readers, but for the institutional respectability backing the *Review*. At any rate Henry wrote a preface to the story, and, with Mr. Faulkner's consent, both were brought out in an edition of 300 copies by the Book Club of Texas, which was sponsored by Stanley Marcus, one of the patrons of the *Southwest Review*.

About the time "Miss Zilphia Gant" appeared, with Henry's illuminating preface, in 1932, Henry was in England, taking a summer course at Oxford University.

At this juncture a personification of intolerance, priggery, hypocritical prudery, and minuscular jealousy attacked him as being too foul-minded for further employment. This will always seem funny to those people acquainted with the cherubic nature of Henry's truthfulness. It is kind of Blake-like. Henry rushed back to America, instituted legal proceedings against being fired, and for some months, until the Board of Trustees met and reinstated him as a teacher, remained on the payroll without any classes and with full time to devote to the *Review*.

In 1953 the same personification of intolerance, prudery, priggery, jealousy, and anti-intellect that tried to fire Henry as a teacher while he was acting as editor launched a new attack on the *Southwest Review*. But despite the more favorable climate which the craze of McCarthyism had created for such an attack, the *Review* came out in 1954, as it had in 1932, in a stronger position and with strengthened respect from responsible people.

On August 12, 1936, Henry wrote me a letter that opened my eyes to the price being paid for maintaining the *Review*.

Keeping the magazine going [he said] seems to involve an outlay of energy and time that is entirely unreasonable; according to all common sense, it is not worth it; and many times we have almost decided to give it up. But usually a sort of mysticism intervenes. When someone asks me why I have worked with the magazine for so long, I am unable to offer a rational explanation. It might be that if we took a firmer stand we could get more money and support from the University or from somewhere else.

For some months this spring and summer, after the

Trustees killed our plan for founding a University Press by bringing up the Faulkner controversy again, McGinnis has been very low in his mind, and I have wondered whether his attitude towards the *Review* has really undergone a fundamental change. Maybe when he gets back from his vacation he will feel more like going on with it, but he was very much depressed when he left. [Artists and writers whom McGinnis saw in New Mexico and Colorado gave him an injection of optimism. Within a few months the University trustees voted to establish the S.M.U. Press, and McGinnis was eager with plans for it.] It would be impossible to carry on without him unless there were some change in the set-up. Before leaving he told me that he proposed to have nothing to do with the magazine any longer unless University authorities gave me a reduction in teaching load so that I might assume most of the responsibility and he serve primarily in an advisory capacity. George Bond, who used to be editor with Hubbell, is back here now working on an M.A. and teaching, but he is so busy he has little time to help with the magazine. He is one of the best editors I ever saw, and if we could have him as editor the problem might be solved.

Observations and theories in Henry's letters constantly reveal his play of mind. Of a young man who was doing some sort of work, the nature of which I never knew, on a Mexican tale about Juan Oso that I sent in, Henry wrote:

If I had known he is going to be so slow, I should have got someone else to do it, but after he had begun I couldn't very well do anything except try to hurry him up. He is a theological student and has some of the Methodist relaxation. The Methodists, it seems to me, have almost entirely escaped being influenced by the Calvinistic attitude, and to this very day have retained a sort of Church of England in-

214 *Out of the Old Rock*

dolence. Once in a while we turn up a crusader, but in the main the Methodist idea is to live and let live. I suppose I prefer this to the Presbyterian earnestness, but it is irritating to work with the Methodists.

Back in 1934, presaging his *Virgin Land: The American West as Symbol and Myth,* published sixteen years later, Henry was writing:

> I do not seem able to stay away from literary theory. . . . I find myself coming back again and again to the subject of myth. It begins to seem to me that the wholly mysterious value of literature may lie principally in its creation and communication of myth. Of course one has to extend the meaning of myth slightly — slightly!! — and to classify, say, the adventures of Becky Sharp as a myth.

A magazine editor necessarily formulates conceptions of the kind of writing he wants to publish, and of proportions. During the interplay of Henry Smith's and John McGinnis's minds I don't know which led on theories about a desirable balance in the magazine between straightaway, often *un-ideal* writings reflecting the Southwest and articles dealing with subjects of worldwide interest. In the fall of 1937, shortly after Henry had left for Harvard and while George Bond was temporarily working with the magazine, I boiled out in a letter to Mac that I decided not to mail. A passage from it will show that I did not agree with all the editorial theories:

> Henry wrote that an essay on coyotes, most of it reminiscences of a pet coyote, by one of my students did not "fit" the magazine. To me it was more interesting and had more vitality than numerous treatises that have seemed to "fit"

the *Review* since the coyote piece was turned down. If writing is interesting and vital, what other fitness does it need?

McGinnis planned farther ahead on the *Review* than on his own conduct. "I have been thinking of coming to see you one day this week," he wrote. "Might get off tonight. In that case I shall see you before this letter arrives." While I was sending the magazine batches of reviews of minor books and pamphlets — all pertaining to the West or Southwest and all, temporarily, interesting to me for fragments of stuff to be utilized in the making of literature — McGinnis casually remarked that he had no ambition to make the *Southwest Review* a rival of the *Southwestern Historical Quarterly*.

We all had lots of fun, and the fun continued after Allen Maxwell began assuming responsibilities in 1938. Along with a sharp sense of humor, he has a kind of Cato mind — the Cato who always ended every oration he made, no matter on what subject, with "Delenda est Carthago!" If Allen Maxwell is after something for the *Review,* or for Southern Methodist University Press, he will hammer for it every time he sees you, no matter where, every time he writes you, no matter about what. "I think," he characteristically wrote in one letter, "that getting a sketch on Lomax out of Bedichek is worth an *infinite amount of urging."* Allen should write down, nothing extenuate, his experiences in drawing material for the *Review* out of John Lomax.

One form of fun has entailed extra work by my editorial comrades. That is having reprints made of certain of my tales and articles published in the *Review*. Giving them away is a special pleasure, particularly those branded for Christmas remembrance. The two

handsomest have been "Juan Oso" (1933) and "A Plot
of Earth" (1953). Henry Smith went to all sorts of pains
on design, paper, cover, et cetera, for "Juan Oso." He and
I had recently made a long pack trip through vast and
empty lands of northern Mexico. I wrote some verses
for the booklet that found no place in the long "Juan
Oso" tale as finally published in *Tongues of the Monte*.
They give me an elation now that associates storytellings
in camps and ridings over mountains and deserts of
Mexico with dear Henry Smith and the *Southwest Review*.

> *It was Christmas Eve in the Sierras,*
>   *We kept the fire piled high.*
> *"Señor, it's true," he said in starting,*
>   *"Tonight no sheep will die."*
>
> *The wind roared down the canyon jags —*
>   *Naught but the tale I heard.*
> *In calmness now the white frost fell,*
>   *And only Juan Oso erred.*
>
> *I saw the Dipper swing around;*
>   *The coyote began his yelling;*
> *A mule arose from his bed of grass.*
>   *The teller kept on telling.*
>
> *The dawn was up and so was I*
>   *When Juan to his palace came.*
> *God bless all lovers of tales —*
>   *It's Christmas once again.*

Allen Maxwell and McGinnis and I, with Tom Lea
as illustrator, had a bully time in 1939 bringing out
my *John C. Duval: First Texas Man of Letters* — one of

only two books published by the *Southwest Review.*
Tom's pictures are gusto personified. Most of the book's
contents had been printed in the magazine and the type
held. It sold for $1.50, and nobody made a nickel out
of it. Earl Vandale, that prince of collectors and en-
courager of writers about the Southwest, bought a hundred copies, at 50 percent discount, to give away. Nobody lost a nickel on the venture. *John C. Duval* is now
a seldom-found item in the rare-book bins.

It was not until after the United States formally entered World War II, a move I had worked for from the
beginning, that I came to agree with McGinnis and
other editors on proportion in the magazine between
our little Southwestern *where* and other *wheres.*

When the *Review* is fifty years old it would be appro-
priate to bring out a volume of the best writings, in all
forms, published in the magazine during the half-cen-
tury of its existence. A qualification for the best will be
the enduring qualities of every piece considered. I nomi-
nate for this 1965* anthology "France's Undeclared
Civil War," by Lon Tinkle, published in the Autumn
number of 1940. This number did not appear until we
were a good deal nearer Pearl Harbor than the date on
the magazine was. At that, the issue was far less behind
in appearing than many other issues had been and were
to be. The lead article was Lon Tinkle's. Not until the
summer of 1955 did I read it, charmed by its urbane
lucidity and enlightened by its realistic comprehension
of the French genius and of political and social movements in France between the two World Wars.

---

* In using this date Dobie includes *Texas Review,* which opened in
1915. The greatly changed *Southwest Review* will be fifty years old
in 1974. — Ed.

As soon as I saw the cover of that issue of the magazine, on a day fifteen years back, without reading anything in it at all I fired off a protest to McGinnis against giving primary editorial emphasis to something about France. Perhaps I should add that I myself had nothing in the magazine, having sent in nothing. Mac retorted:

I'm not upset at your objection to our international article. I defend my point of view by saying that *at the moment* not cotton, nor your Nueces County cows — certainly not recollections of Texas yesteryears — can be considered as important to Texans — urban or rural — as whether we shall fall into the democratic confusion that finished France, and almost got England. I simply couldn't face the criticism — the potential criticism — that might be made now or years later: "The poor sand-blind Regionalists didn't realize what was happening to them," or, "The nation's fate was at stake, and they were talking about little regional books and prints."

Few men in whom the tides of life run strong can fix change in philosophy on a given hour, place, or person as John Bunyan reckoned the change in his life from the hour when, while he was tinkering with a pot, he heard some women sitting in the sun "talk about the things of God." I was not immediately converted to the McGinnis standard of values for the magazine. Several months after his bull's-eye hit, I wrote Henry Smith: "I am all for making the *Review* a little less international and more local than the last number is." Just the same, about this time I began to become a contemporary of my own times. Before that, the pageant of the past and the flavor of the present derived from the past were all-sufficient for me. Most analyses of problems bored me — and still do, for thinking is unnatural to me, whereas the pictures and conversation favored by Alice are natural. I never did want the *Review* to express the county mind; I have always felt a distrust of regionalism as a cult; my ideal regionalist has all along been Shakespeare. When the magazine came out in 1947 with an article on the right to think, "Are Professors Dangerous?" by Clarence Ayres, I told Allen Maxwell that his magazine would be distinguished if it had nothing else, and that any magazine now contenting itself with tradition in manners and customs would be an antiquity. While the profit-motivated were proclaiming themselves as sublime and were warring to suppress thought and intellect, prating on the Texas tradition became sawdusty.

It seems to me that the *Review*'s concern during these latter years with what Allen Maxwell calls "the condition of intellectual freedom" in Texas and elsewhere has been a highly proper form of regionalism. I shall go on honing for flavor and color and lusty life — and I salute, with profound gratitude, intellectual integrity and the stand for the liberalism that goes with enlightenment by the present editorial direction of the *Southwest Review. The Moving Finger writes; and, having writ, moves on.**

---

* Decherd Turner was editor from 1963 to 1965; Margaret Hartley has been editor from 1965 to the present time. She had served as assistant editor (from 1947 to 1961) and managing editor (from 1961 to 1963) while Allen Maxwell was editor. — Ed.

E. Douglas Branch, Singularísimo

> I like odd characters. I am one.
> — BALZAC
> How glorious it is — and also
> how painful — to be an exception.
> — DE MUSSET

EDWARD Douglas Branch was born in Houston, Texas, July 7, 1905; he had a younger brother and two sisters. The family was of Methodist persuasion, although I never heard him express an interest in any church, and certainly after he got away from home he never entered one to worship. For that matter, I never heard him even allude to his father, whom he resembled closely in both physical and intellectual qualities. The founder of the Branch family in Texas came from Virginia in 1833, fought in the Battle of San Jacinto, was elected to the first Congress of the Republic of Texas, and then became a member of the Republic's Supreme Court. Edward Thomas (commonly called Tom) Branch, Douglas's father, began working in a bookstore at the age of twelve and "devoured the stock day and night." A fragile, little man, he read law, had a prodigious memory, became one of the most distinguished members of the Texas bar, recodified the criminal laws of the state, wrote law books, and without monetary compensation saw Branch's *Annotated Penal Code* (Chicago, 1916) become the "Bible" of criminal courts and trial lawyers over Texas. Revised and enlarged in 1956, it remains "the Bible."

After graduating from a Houston high school, Douglas entered the University of Texas in January, 1922. He was a sophomore when he registered for my class in English 3 in September following. The record shows that all his grades at Texas were good except for an F in Physical Training — due no doubt to his refusal to recognize the existence of that compulsory course.

English 3 was an advanced course in composition wherein we studied Genung's *Rhetoric,* paid attention to grammar, and drilled on the architecture of sentences. The pupils read a good deal and wrote essays and narratives. They were not timid in criticizing each other's papers. This class of fourteen was the most distinguished in quality of individuals that I directed in my whole academic career. There was Anita Brenner, whose *Idols Behind Altars* and other books interpretive of Mexico hold up well. The most mature mind in the class, not excluding the instructor's, was that of Prussian-born Hartmann Dignowity, who knew Goethe, Darwin, Nietzsche, Wagner, and Shakespeare, but needed to perfect his use of the English language. He considered Branch an amusing infant with perhaps more pretensions than powers. Another member of the class, Leeper Gay, introduced me to a character named Wes Burton across the River — the Colorado River — who had dedicated his life to hunting the Lost San Saba Mine. Wes and his parents and sister were storybook characters and led me a long way into what became the book entitled *Coronado's Children.*

I was at the time probably experimenting more in the craft of writing than any of my pupils. After being in the Field Artillery in World War I for about two years, I had come back to the University of Texas as an instructor, taught for a year, resigned to manage a big ranch down in the Brush Country, and now was back again among the academicians. My pupils were fresh human beings to me; Branch remains in my memory as the nearest to a genius I ever had.

He was delicate in body and limb, maybe not over five feet two or three inches tall, hardly weighing over 130 pounds. His complexion was of a virginal rose; he did not yet need to shave and had no down. He kept his black hair brushed flat. His eyes, somewhat protruding, were extraordinarily bright and flashed when he was interested — as he habitually was. The talk was that he burned sandalwood in his room in order to inhale the fragrance. He would have burned mesquite or anything else in order to enjoy the reputation of being a character. I had read with avidity *The Confessions of an English Opium Eater* and saw in Branch a veritable simulacrum of De Quincey.

He had a disdain for pedestrian minds and announced himself a woman-hater. One of his class essays burned with contempt for perfumes used by young women to disguise other odors. To regard Branch's slight figure and then to hear his bass voice was to be startled even after one knew him well. That voice was his passport to virility, though he was never garrulous and was quiet in conversation. He tended to reserve his booms for effect, just as he came to smoke a long, black cigar in public. Wilfred Scawen Blunt said of Nietzsche, promoter of the doctrine of Teutonic superiority: "He admires

strength because he is physically a weakling. He despises
women because he does not know them." I never had
much affection for Branch, but he was interesting to me
forty years ago and has been interesting to me ever since.
Here I shall quote from reminiscences of Branch kindly
written down for me by my friend Hartmann Dignowity.

His knowledge of literature awed everyone in our class,
including, I believe, Mr. Dobie. One day I found him in
the library looking through catalogue cards and writing
down titles of books by authors mentioned in an essay we
were reading. He was not embarrassed to confide in me
that should Mr. Dobie ask questions about these writers —
as was his habit — he could by glibly rattling off titles of
their works leave the impression that he was familiar with
them. Dobie stopped me one day on the campus and commented on Branch's wide knowledge of past and contemporary literature. I did not give Branch away.

His physical appearance almost conditioned his attitudes.
A "pince nez" secured by a black ribbon around his neck
was such an obvious affectation that girls giggled when
they saw him — but hardly ever gave him a second look.
Walking through the state capitol one time, we were about
to pass an old woman soliciting funds for crippled and sick
children when she addressed her appeal to him. He adjusted
his glasses, looked straight into her eyes and said: "I am
adamant. Let the children die," and walked on. To me the
play was most amusing. The old woman very likely did not
know what *adamant* meant, but that word, look, and gesture left her gasping.

At Zerchausky's, a near-beer garden, once the Bismarck
Saloon, he would order beer and rye bread with cheese or
German sausage. I always felt that his drinking and eating
there were affectation from a desire to appear masculine.
He was not eager to pay for our repasts. His favorite author
at this time was Ambrose Bierce.

One could not take the B.A. degree at the University of Texas without credit for mathematics or, as a substitute for mathematics, Greek. In the fall of 1923 Branch went to the State University of Iowa, where academic requirements were more to his liking. He received the B.A. degree in the spring of 1924 and the M.A. a year later. His chief mentor at Iowa was Louis Pelzer, professor of American history, who directed his M.A. thesis, entitled "The Historical Foundations of the Fiction of the Ranch and Range." Pelzer showed a copy of the thesis to a representative of D. Appleton and Company. In the fall of 1926 that publisher brought out *The Cowboy and His Interpreters,* by Douglas Branch. Branch gave me to understand that the book is substantially the thesis.

He did not want the public to know that the author was a twenty-one-year-old academician who had probably never been on a ranch and who would have been wretched had he been forced to live and work on one. He had asked me to write an introduction. I sent it. The publishers, he replied, said that it "would ruin" him. He seemed relieved by their decision not to use the introduction. They were advertising him as "born and raised in the heart of the cow country." Perhaps only cow people would know from what is not said as well as from what is said in the book that he had never associated with cows, followed a cow trail, or drunk water out of a cow track. The best of imaginations can flourish in authenticity only through a mastery of facts. What I said that "would ruin" the book was later put into a review, from which I quote: "Douglas Branch is not a cowboy, and is the first Texan to interpret cowboys without claiming to be one." While pointing out specific misrepresentations, I said much in favor of the book. It remains readable and valid.

A college lad could not be expected to produce a mature book, but Branch was an intellectual and was already enjoying play of mind upon any subject that he treated of. He did not know life and therefore could not be expected to know cowboys. He was moving toward a critical attitude. "There was no driving to do; the cattle moved of their own free will as in ordinary travel." Thus Branch quotes from Andy Adams's *The Log of a Cowboy*. Then he observes: "And the narrative itself seems to move of its own free will — leisurely, sure of itself, as natural as the trail men themselves. There are no grim, firm-lipped heroes among them, engrossed in their own humorless melodramas. Zane Grey would not know what to do with them." Branch is freer, and therefore better, interpreting the interpreters than the cowboys themselves. It is fine to prance when you are twenty, but pretense is something else. After all, as compared to the pretenses of piety and greed, the pretense of having sweated in a cowpen is very innocent.

During 1923–1925 I was head of the English department at Oklahoma A. & M. College. In the summer of 1925 I gave Branch his first teaching job. To the descendants of Oklahoma squatters he was an oddity beyond their world, but for all I know they got along well enough together. He had a fellowship the following academic year at Ohio State University. He was working on the buffalo; also, to quote a letter of December 9, 1925, "reading such stuff as Strabo and Lucian, and smoking prodigiously." The following April he summed up his gainings in Columbus thus: "Material for the buffalo opus, four or five acquaintances, and bronchitis." Notice his precision in saying acquaintances rather than friends. He was hoping to get a job teaching history at the University of Texas or some other university to the west.

What he got was the professorship of American history at Louisiana Industrial Institute at Ruston — $3,-000, 130 students, and "I am my own department." He was feeling his oats. To quote from a Louisiana letter: "I had a note from Andy Adams designating me as the chief of his many press agents." (This is an allusion to *The Cowboy and His Interpreters*.) "I thought that if the eminent Andy could afford to insert the word *many* I could afford not to answer the note." He had been to New York and in a Shubert revue seen "nudes that were not nudes but simply so much meat . . ."

In 1927–1928 he was back at the State University of Iowa, where in June of 1928 he was granted the Ph.D. — the youngest recipient, it has been said, of the degree in that university's history. His thesis was on "The Utilization, Recession, and Near-Extermination of the American Bison." Under title of *The Hunting of the Buffalo* it was published by Appleton in January, 1929. Branch had decided that his name would carry more weight if it had an initial prefixed to it; from now on his books were by E. Douglas Branch. Branch knew that he was writing a book and not a thesis. The buffalo book is more mature than *The Cowboy and His Interpreters*. Here scoffing has developed into irony. "I trust you," he wrote, "to keep to yourself in any review the circumstance that the book is my Ph.D. thesis (reannotated, but hardly changed otherwise)."

It was absurd for Branch to take Pawnee Bill — perhaps the most flushing four-flusher yet produced by Oklahoma — as a consultant on the buffalo. Not to

recognize downright Charles Goodnight as a main pre-
server of the buffalo was an error. Branch was still short
of twenty-four years of age when the book was published.
It transmutes skeletons into vitalities. Here once more
the buffalo bull paws into the earth, bellows his chal-
lenges, and before his countless followers fights in mighty
pride for life and leadership; once more the great fur
companies compete in trading knives and whiskey for
pemmican and robes; once more the Plains warriors
make their great surrounds on foot, then run down cows
and bulls on Spanish horses. I would say that no better
introduction to Branch at his best can be found than his
gusto over Captain Meriwether Lewis's description of
the cooking and eating of *boudin blanc*. Gusto, sympathy for the subject, is not a common virtue. Branch
had it, and sophistication never killed it in his writings.
He never wrote a dull page or a fulsome sentence.

The year *The Hunting of the Buffalo* was published,
Branch was in residence at the University of Iowa, living
on a grant from the Social Science Research Council.
He was trying to locate a good teaching job. In July,
1928, he reported an advance of $1,800 by Appleton for
a "popular but substantial" history of the West. He had
office space with Louis Pelzer and a free run of the
library, where, as Professor Ross Livingston remembers,
"He would often spend all night working. He was kindly
receptive to suggestions any professor made about his
work, or even his personal appearance. On one occasion
I explained to him that being small, short, and frail, he
should select clothing that would not accentuate those
characteristics. I suggested blunt-pointed collars, large
ties, coats with short lapels, hat creased flat. When I saw
him at a professional meeting in Des Moines some time

later, he had adopted some of my suggestions and good-humoredly asked me to look him over."

Like all of us, Branch responded kindly to kindness and was more humble-minded than many gave him credit for being. "You may be amazed to hear it," he said out loud in a letter of 1929, "but I have some modesty, and I don't expect to write — or be able to write — a first-rate book for half a dozen years yet."

At the same time he could say: "I'm profoundly convinced of the truth of my own prejudices only in matters of literary principles. I hate Dreiser, Suckow, and Harriet Monroe with a beautiful and holy hate — with James Joyce and Zane Grey in the tier just below them."

After a final examination in contemporary American fiction at Iowa, as his instructor John T. Frederick recollects, Branch "expressed his opinion of one of the books assigned (Ruth Suckow's *Country People*) by tearing his copy to bits and depositing them in a wastebasket up front — to the excitement of the class." He was never, understand, a book-burner — but Cyrano de Bergerac was one of his admirations. "What a gesture!"

"A career as historian of the West may not be what I would have chosen; it may not be the thing I'm best suited for. But I shall tackle this history of the West honestly and with a little humility." Thus Branch viewed himself soon after accepting $1,800 to carry out his editor's idea of a book. Before it got published — and neglected — he was (May 16, 1929) proposing a life of Ramsay Crooks of the American Fur Company. What became of that project is unknown to me.

Westward, a not-wordy book of around 200,000 words running to 627 pages, counting the index, appeared in 1930. The Great Depression had struck, and Branch nevcr recovered from the blow. About a year following publication of *Westward,* he wrote me: "When I survey that unwieldy edifice I feel three kinds of a fool. The fact that I was sick as a pup summer before last is no excuse for my having dodged the simple drudgery of verification that would have made it nearly a first-rate book. I wonder if anybody ever learns anything."

The book is better than Branch rated it, though not well proportioned. It starts in with "when Massachusetts was West," but hardly gets to the end of the nineteenth century. Here, as elsewhere, Branch is particular, concrete, selective of detail; I used to quote Blake to the class he was in: "To generalize is to be an idiot. Knowledge consists of particulars." To me, the first part of *Westward* is fresher, more vivid than the latter, which takes in the Wild West.

A new field for Branch was women. Early in 1929 he wrote, rather simperingly I thought, of a young lady in Washington who had made an impression upon his heart. She was not the Perla whom he married and with whom he was living in New York in 1931, hard up for money and a job. According to one of his friends, she was "capable"; according to another, bride and groom were both attractive. "He was extremely well groomed, sharp featured, and had clear, keen eyes back of modest, rimless spectacles. His wife was nothing short of beautiful. She was properly demure, as the wife of a successful rising young author, with an oral mastery of historical wisdom and a genius at phrase-making, should be. All in all, our evening with the couple was very, very pleasant. Nevertheless, it was apparent that a sharp tongue and oracular opinionation were his worst enemies."

In March of 1932 Douglas's mother wrote me from

Houston asking that I try to find a job for him. I had tried; there were no jobs. She said that he was "beginning to assume an inferiority complex," that his parents were educating another son and could hardly spare more money to Douglas. In a jaunty letter received from him a few days earlier he spoke in an offhand way of reviewing books for "Cole." My expressing ignorance of the editor brought this retort:

The "Cole" whose name I used with a familiarity you found arrant is simply the editor of the *Mississippi Valley Historical Review,* which quarterly I humbly assumed you read once in a while. As for the editors of publications that pay money to their authors, I am sorrowful (as a homeless author) and proud (as a gentleman) that I don't know any. I have met quite a few, but that's something else again.

If Perla and I can, by some sheer miracle of the "dismal science," provide ourselves with bed and board, I shall have completed, by the first of June, my masterpiece; my relict can pay for her weeds with the royalties. The book will begin with the Great Fire of December 16, 1835, in New York City and conclude at about the time Mr. George B. Jocelyn, railroad agent of Vincennes, Indiana, wrote the three social degrees (Love, Equality and Fraternity) of the Knights Templars. Since I cannot find a market, I had as well do what I want to do, and write a good book.

The "good book" Branch was to complete by the first of June did not get published until 1934. By then Perla had divorced him and become a security officer for a chain of stores. Meanwhile Branch's publishers had through a merger become D. Appleton–Century Company. The title of the book is *The Sentimental Years: 1836–1860.*

As *Westward* is a social history with emphasis on

place and time, *The Sentimental Years* is a social history with emphasis on people — their manners, hypocrisies, greeds, credulities, also sincerities and other attributes. Rich in irony, wit, and urbanity, vivid in Macaulay-like details, deft in craftsmanship, it is Branch's ripest work. Here he is sophisticated where sophistication fits. Compassion has come to him; patronization has gone away.

"The machinery of government was intrusted to a convenient element, the professional politicians — who maintained themselves by being professional democrats." John Bartholomew Gough, firebrand of the Temperance Movement, "offered a creed of self-perfectibility by perfecting the conduct of other people." Textile laborers in Massachusetts worked eleven hours a day. In an election year "the Hamilton Company had a notice posted on the factory gate: 'Whoever, employed by this corporation, votes the Ben Butler Ten-Hour ticket will be discharged.'" In the South, Scott's *Ivanhoe* "coddled the illusion of a second age of chivalry."

Probably the most congenial position of Branch's life was as associate professor of English and history at Montana State University (called also University of Montana) at Missoula. Here he found a friend in Professor Harold Merriam, with whom he enjoyed editing *Frontier and Midland*. "An excellent gentleman," he characterized Merriam to me, "but a frustrated idealist, hence of unpredictable whim." It was hard for him to resist a lance. I don't know if he ever loved anybody; he truly liked his friend and mentor Louis Pelzer and realized a debt to him, but this remark was passed around as a Branch cut: "I wrote my thesis under a wooden-minded professor who didn't know a social significance from a whirlwind."

In September, 1936, "on a postman's holiday in Missoula," he wrote: "I lost something of human peace and quite a little divinity under my feet by leaving Montana (in the fall of 1935) for a full professorship and a meet wage at the Cathedral of Learning" (the University of Pittsburgh in a skyscraper). While in Pittsburgh he was for a time paid secretary of the Historical Society of Western Pennsylvania. His published books — four in nine years — were all behind him. At the age of twenty-nine his writing career was over.

On August 10, 1939, he sent out the following announcement from Pittsburgh, Pennsylvania:

On Friday, July 28, 1939, at Winchester, Virginia, Dr. E. Douglas Branch and one Helen Schmidt, an excellent and comely person, were united to mutual gratulations.

The immediately present family comprises one Kitten which sleeps with us, and three Turtles which do not.

Dr. Branch regrets that a broken right hand precludes his scribbling, for a few weeks, the personal amenities which accompany this message.

That hand gave him increasing trouble. The "excellent and comely person" was a grass widow with a child. On July 4, 1942 — and it had been a long time between letters — he wrote me from Chicago:

I left the gilded hypocrisy of Pittsburgh almost coincidentally with our entrance into the war. Am 4-F myself, thanks to two (the maximal quota per person, I believe) broken hands: no actual handicap, save that I cannot lift and carry anything. I've been working on a couple of "patriotic" programs at CBS here.

I have become a Number One aillurophile [defined in the next letter as a cat-lover], specializing in confused breeds; we have three beautiful bastards now.

That *we* would indicate that the "excellent and comely person" with whom he and "one Kitten" were sleeping in 1939 was still the wife of Dr. E. Douglas Branch. She did not so remain much longer. About this time he went west again for a year with Montana State College at Bozeman.

Before this he had, among historians of the Midwest, become a kind of legend for brilliance — soon to be of brilliance and drink in the Edgar Allan Poe pattern. His presence at any meeting of the Mississippi Valley Historical Association was marked. "At midnight the year the M.V.H.A. met at Vincennes," to quote Walker D. Wyman of Wisconsin State College. "Branch had not yet written a paper to be delivered the following day. By ten the next morning it was down on paper — in publishable form."

In the fall of 1945 he got a part-time teaching job with Roosevelt University, supplemented by one with the Chicago Undergraduate Division of the University of Illinois. His work at Roosevelt warranted his being given a special course in the spring term. Within two months he was missing so many classes or showing up in such a state of incoherent drunkenness that there was "no alternative to releasing him." Off and on during the forties he ground out articles for the *American Peoples Encyclopedia* in Chicago under the editorship of Franklin J. Meine, writing "a large part of the American history material in the early volumes." Too much alcoholism lost him this connection, but his work — astonishingly rapid — was so excellent that the *Encyclopedia* put up with him even after he was no longer dependable.

For part of the academic year 1946–1947 his flickering

candle made a — locally — fine light at Center College,
Danville, Kentucky. The following is from a recorded
interview with John Hakac, presently with the University of Arizona.

That year I was taking Freshman English under a couple
of jackasses at Center. Dr. Branch had the maturest and
brightest students in a Shakespeare course. He was a cele-
brated campus character. Danville was dry, but Lexington,
forty miles away, wasn't. A bus that left Lexington about 2
A.M. on Sunday mornings was usually loaded with more or
less drunken students. Frequently Dr. Branch would climb
and stumble aboard among them, always carrying a leather
satchel making *clink, clink, clink* sounds. Some student
would ask, "What do you have there, Dr. Branch?" He
would reply, "Records," and ride back to Danville in a stu-
por.

He wore army clothes, GI olive drabs, even a khaki tie.
Some students declared that he went a month without
changing his clothes; dress in no way dented his appeal.
They loved him, sympathized with him. When we heard
that Dr. Branch was the author of books, we undergraduates
ran to the library to gaze upon a book by a man who walked
among us in the flesh. One student declared *The Hunting
of the Buffalo* good reading but objectionable on account
of the punctuation. He had counted twenty-six semicolons,
he said, on one page. They interrupted his interest. Periods
would have been all right. Faulkner, without any punctuation at all, would have been better.

Dr. Branch was living alone in one room. According to
student belief, his wife had died in a fire and his resultant
suffering was so great that he took to the bottle and lived
in utter loneliness.

The end of the semester (1947) came and Branch had not
turned in his final grades. The deadline passed and still no
grades were in. I'm just telling what was common talk. The

college dean went to Branch's room and knocked on the
door. He got no answer, walked in anyhow, and found Dr.
Branch drunk in bed. Rousing him slightly, he asked if the
final grades were ready. Dr. Branch said no. "Get up and
get those grades. We need them," the dean admonished.
Branch remained supine. The dean now suggested that he
would read the class roll and Branch could say off A, B,
C, D, etc. as an estimated grade. Branch agreed. Most of the
class were GI's. Finally the dean came to a Mr. Smith. "I
can't recall that name at all," Branch said. The dean identified Mr. Smith in some way. "Oh, yes," Branch cried, "I
remember him now. Give him an A — poor devil, he's married."

Back in Chicago, to which he always returned, Branch
tried to get a counter job with the Thompson restaurant
chain. He had worked irregularly in Chicago restaurants
before this. His borrowings had cut him off from nearly
all acquaintances in the teaching world. Now he failed
to pass the required physical examination. During this
period he got a job in some West Virginia college, but
it didn't last. Occasionally he reviewed a book for the
Chicago *Sun*. His shirts and suits became seedier, his
skin more flushed, his hands more tremulous, his nervous sweat more profuse, his deep voice out of such a
small and wasted body more haunting. Professor Kendall B. Taft, of Roosevelt University, solicited and obtained aid for him from writing men over the nation.
Branch had cut his hand on a bread slicer in some greasy
spoon. From now on he would have no respite from
Skid Row, sometimes washing dishes in cheap eating
places, sometimes serving at the counter, sometimes
waiting on tables, sometimes just sitting. In response to
one letter written during his long, long downhill stum-

bling I sent money to buy a cheap suit of clothes. According to his report, something happened to the suit — if the few dollars went for it. The following letter tells all one needs to know about Grub Street existence in one American city by one ruined writer.

Dear J. Frank:

I am in most rarefiedly refreshed mood, just having read Eudora Welty's *The Robber Bridegroom* for the first time, and raptly.

I began the New Year auspiciously by picking up a banner (translation: responding to a "Waiter Wanted" sign in the window) at 1 A.M., January the first, and I surmise I may do as well at 10 tonight, since I have seen a waiter due to take up his shift there who has taken up too much already.

Thank goodness I am nimble, if I have no strength. There is so little I can do, of the work arrantly (and mistakenly) called "unskilled." What chance I had for a college appointment last fall was effectively wrecked by the collusion of the College Specialists Bureau and the Chicago postoffice.

I have so much to write, and see so little likelihood that I shall. But this is 1950; the thrice broken right hand may almost be called dextrous again, and the sinister hand has acquired dexterity.

My rent and my larder run four days ahead at the moment, which is good. One week in October, after a hebdomad of inanition to give my coccyx opportunity to half-forget my annual Slip on the Ice, I spent three nights of five as a non-ordering table-sitter in various restaurants where I am known; and I have learned that the only thing really to dread is to be utterly out of tobacco.

The smug Babbitts who think of "clerical positions" and the like have no realization that bed and food are not sal vered instanter on the first day, that swans do not furnish one with eider nor ravens with matzoth, to bridge the appalling gap until the first check. Random catering, with the hope of a culinary liaison of duration (and how little turnover there is now! How rabid and hungry the competition!) — the horizon goes little farther. Sans contract; sans lectern or swivel.

But there are worse. And I read until I know it an opiate. The very best of 1950 for you.

Douglas

On July 18, 1954, I was in Missoula, Montana. The *Daily Missoulian* of that morning printed an Associated Press dispatch from Helena saying that Dr. E. Douglas Branch, former instructor at Montana State University and Montana State College, had died in Chicago July 10, three days after his forty-ninth birthday. Several years before this he had virtually disappeared from the world that once knew him.

I can summon no better end than a paragraph in a letter from his friend Kendall B. Taft of Roosevelt University:

His is a genuinely tragic fall of valor. To one who knew Douglas at his best, there could be no question about his brilliance, his wit, and his potential charm. He had a remarkable, though brief, period of productivity. Where the flaw lay, I do not know. His alcoholism was very probably a symptom, rather than a basic cause, of his moral deterioration. I do not judge him, God knows, but have only a profound regret that one so gifted should have been defeated — for whatever cause — by the demands of life.